TO THE FOLKS BACK HOME
Echoes of The Great War

Mansfield Area Historical Society

Copyright © 2025 Mansfield Area Historical Society
All cover art copyright © 2025 Mansfield Area Historical Society
All Rights Reserved

No part of this book may be reproduced or transmitted in any form or by any means, electronic or mechanical, including photocopying, recording, or by any information storage and retrieval system, without permission in writing from the author.

(Cover photo Courtesy of the Bob Davis family)

Publishing Coordinator – Sharon Kizziah-Holmes

Paperback-Press
an imprint of A & S Publishing
Paperback Press, LLC
Springfield, Missouri

ISBN -13: 978-1-964559-81-0 Paperback
ISBN: 13: 978-1-964559-82-7 Hardback

DEDICATION

To the World War One veterans of Wright County, Missouri, and the other area counties for their extreme acts of bravery in service to our country and to their families who endured the anguish of separation from their loved ones.

A special tribute to Clarence King, Mansfield's first WWI casualty, and to all the Wright County heroes who gave their lives:

Charley A. Ball, Palmer F. Ball, Roy W. Bare, Frank Beckett, Otto F. Binkley, Harley W. Bragg, James M. Branstetter, Jesse Brazeal, Lloyd D. Breckner, Charles T. Carter, James C. Chadwell, Alexander Clark, Jess Crisp, Oscar A. Denton, Glen H. Edwards, Joseph F. Evans, George E. Findley, Samuel D. Floyd, Alva Gartin, Paul E. Gresham, Chessley Hire, Orville A. Hofford, Ault Hunt, John W. Hunt, Thomas C. Ingraham, Louis W. Johnson, Clarence King, Yaroslov Liska, Oliver H. McMurtrey, Clarence Plaster, James B. Scott, Elmer O. Sellers, James W. Skiles, Henry I. Snow, Walter G. Street, Leon R. Tester, Maynard H. Thorne, Joseph Todd, Archie Tool, Frank A. Wright, Otis Yeager, Ray Young,

(Listed above are the names as they appear on the "Lest We Forget" granite markers on the lawn of the Wright County Courthouse in Hartville, MO.)

TABLE OF CONTENTS

Dedication 3
Acknowledgments 5
Introduction 6
Notes to the Readers 8
Mansfield's First Casualty 2
April 1918 – November 1918 12
Travel Dates of Company "A" 110th Engineers 92
Post-War Happenings 94
Home at Last 98
Military Abbreviations 100
Military Biographies 101
The Mansfield Area Historical Society 157
Index 158

ACKNOWLEDGMENTS

The purpose of this book is to serve as a chronological account of the lives of the servicemen of Wright County, Missouri, and its surrounding counties, including their letters back home, war events, and local and national happenings.

This book would not have been possible without the collaborative efforts of Vicki Blankenship, Ann Duckworth, and Kathy Short; the officers and board members of the Mansfield Area Historical Society and Museum; the members of the community for their donations of family artifacts and information; and the sources as designated throughout the book.

We would like to express special gratitude to the family members of Clarence King for all the pictures and information that they provided.

Throughout the book, but especially in the biography section, we have strived to enter accurate information. However, in many cases, we found conflicting details, depending on the source and the frequency of the given names. Furthermore, we could find little or no information on some of the people that we were researching, especially when attempting to link them to this area of the state. If we felt that the details were too conflicting, we did not use them. For this reason some of the names mentioned on the monuments and in the pictures are not included in the biography section.

"June 5 will be observed as a holiday in Mansfield in honor of the boys who register, some of whom will be selected to go to war and protect the Stars and Stripes." (*Mansfield Mirror* May 31, 1917)

INTRODUCTION

For authenticity's sake in this book, all letters and information from the *Mansfield Mirror,* as found in *Chronicling America,* were transcribed in their original forms with no grammatical corrections.

The letter selection process for this book was difficult, and we regret that not all letters could be included. However, we hope these excerpts will serve as a glimpse into the lives of and the war contributions made by our own heroes and all those whose names and records may be missing or incomplete.

(Courtesy of the MAHS Collection)

Registration day June 15, 1917 in the Mansfield Park. The backdrop for this picture was J.W. Gilley's big American flag.

(Courtesy of the MAHS Collection)

J. W. Gilley

Born 3-13-1842 – Died 6-25-1926

He was the son of Editha Gilley and served in the Union Army 24th MO Infantry. He had an incredibly large US flag that he would bring to area patriotic events, including the military drafts.

Notes to the Readers

The assassination of Archduke Franz Ferdinand of Prussia and his wife Sophie, heirs to the Austro-Hungarian Empire, on July 28, 1914, started a domino effect that served as the immediate catalyst leading to the beginning of the Great War. Germany declared war on Russia and France in early August 1914. Americans, up to this point, had been against joining the war, wishing to remain neutral and to keep their sons out of harm's way. The underlying factors of entangling alliances due to the marriages of European powers, nationalism, militarism, and imperial rivalries led to conflicts. The major players in The Great War were the Axis/Central Powers and the Allies. The Central Powers included Germany, Austria-Hungary, Bulgaria, and the Ottoman Empire. The Allies included Great Britain, France, Russia, Italy, and the USA.

On May 7, 1915, German submarines torpedoed the British ocean liner, the *RMS Lusitania*, which was suspected of carrying weapons to the British. The ship went down in 18 minutes. This attack killed 1,199 people, including 128 United States citizens. President Woodrow Wilson warned Kaiser Wilhelm II to stop his submarines from attacking American citizens.

However, in 1917 British intelligence intercepted a secret telegram, known as the Zimmerman Telegram, in which Germany made an offer to help Mexico regain some of the territories that it had lost during the Mexican American War of 1846. German forces then proceeded to use their submarines to sink ten United States merchant ships. The subsequent change in public opinion in the United States then convinced President Wilson to declare war on Germany on April 6, 1917.

BASIC MILITARY INFORMATION

The four branches of our military were Army, Navy, Marines, and Guards. American troops were known as the AEF (American Expeditionary Forces). The Great War was not called World War I until after World War II was named.

- An army corps is 60,000 men.
- An infantry division is 10,000 men.
- An infantry brigade is 7,000 men.
- A regiment of infantry is 3,600 men.
- A battalion is 1,000 men.
- A company is 250 men.

- A platoon is 60 men.
- A corporal's squad is 11 men.
- A field artillery brigade comprises 1,300 men.
- A field artillery has 195 men.
- A firing squad is 20 men.
- A supply train has 283 men.

A machine gun battalion has 296 men.

An engineers' regiment has 1,098 men.

An ambulance company has 66 men.

A field hospital has 55 men.

A medicine attachment has 13 men.

A major general leads the field army and also each army corps.

A brigadier general heads each infantry brigade.

A colonel heads each regiment.

A lieutenant colonel is next to rank below a colonel.

A major heads a battalion.

A captain heads a company.

A lieutenant heads a platoon.

A sergeant is next below a lieutenant.

--*Des Moines Capital*

Draft registration occurred in four phases:

Phase I – June 5, 1917 - June 5, 1918, all men 21-31 years of age

Phase II – June 5, 1918 - Sept. 12, 1918, all men who turned 21 since the first phase

Phase III – Sept. 12, 1918 – conclusion of the war, all men 18-45 years of age

Phase IV – Oct. 1918 to the end of the war – Automatic Replacement – New draftees with minimal training were sent to replace casualties.

Honoring Our Fallen

On November 3, 1917, three of General Jack Pershing's men died in the war when Germans raided an Allied camp near Verdun. All three were buried there in northeastern France. Pershing believed that there was no greater glory than for the fallen to be buried in the battlefield with their fallen comrades. Former President Theodore Roosevelt and his wife Edith felt the same way when their son Quentin, an American pilot, was shot down over France and was buried with full military honors by German troops.

However, many American families wanted their sons to be returned to them, so the War Department surveyed the family of each soldier as to whether their son's remains would be returned to the States or buried in the new American military cemeteries in Europe.

In 1920, the United States began the process of recovering the remains, a process that took two years and over $30 million. The bodies of 46,000 were returned to the States while another 30,000 were buried in the cemeteries of Europe. (www.historynet.com/rest-in-peace-bringing-home-u-s-war-dead)

...And Our Story Begins

MANSFIELD'S FIRST CASUALTY

MRS. MARY JANE KING'S BOYS GO TO WAR

Pictured above are Clarence King, Mansfield's first WWI war casualty, and his older brother, Elbert.
(Courtesy of the King family)

Mansfield's American Legion Chapter is named in honor of Clarence King, our first war casualty. Although the Armistice was signed the 11th hour of the 11th day of the 11th month in 1918, it was not until the following week that the *Mansfield Mirror* carried the news of eighteen-year-old Clarence King's death.

Death Notice from the War Department to Mary Jane King Slate Dated 20 Dec 1918

American Expeditionary Forces

Headquarters Services of Supply

Office of the Chief Quartermaster, A.E.F.

Graves Registration Service

From: Chief, Graves Registration Service, American E. F.

To: Mrs. M. J. King, Mansfield, MO

Subject: Place of Burial

Private Clarence King, Co. I, 140th Infantry

Died: 10/16/18

Buried: French Military Cemetery Deuxnoues, Heuse

I am sure that you will pardon the use of a form letter such as we are sending to-day, when you try to realize under what great stress this office is working in order to give as prompt advice as possible concerning facts which are of such very vital importance to our sorrowing friends, whose brave men have suffered martyrdom on battlefields within our sphere of European operation.

It is with great sorrow that I am writing you, and only the urgency of your desire to know, prompts me to push forward this notification when my note is required to be so formal because of the great number to which my name has to be signed. You have probably already received official advice concerning the death of the one whom you gave to your country and the world for the saving of civilization.

You will be comforted in knowing that his body has been recovered, that it lies buried in a spot which is under our care and control, and that there will be no danger of its loss or neglect.

We are sending you, herewith, a note which gives general answers to a number of questions which our bereaved friends are often asking, and it will probably give information concerning some of the things you are anxious to understand.

Please be sure of our earnest desire to guard your interests in every possible way, and our satisfaction in being able to care for the resting places of our dead.

Charles C. Pierce
Lieut. Colonel, G.M.C., U.S.A.

America Enters the War

1917

Although the United States' involvement in the Great War, which later became known as World War I, began in April 1917 with the Declaration of War on Germany by President Woodrow Wilson and Congress, the first mention of it in the *Mansfield Mirror* was found in the May 31st issue that announced Registration Day. All men 21 to 31 years of age were to be included. This was mandatory, and the penalty for failing to do so was one year in jail. Missouri's quota was 1,240 men; however, Wright County was to supply 36 men, which was based on 2 men per 1,000 population.

Registration Day was set to be held June 5, 1917, in Mansfield from 7:00 a.m. to 9:00 p.m. This event yielded 108 plus 23 absentee registrants. The day was celebrated as a holiday with townsfolk and countryfolk alike gathering in the park to enjoy patriotic speeches and music provided by the Mansfield Concert Band.

Patriotic gathering in the Mansfield Park Square.
(Courtesy of the MAHS Collection)

The Mansfield Concert Band
(Courtesy of the MAHS Collection)

Each registrant was presented with a badge, courtesy of the *Mansfield Mirror*. The opportunity to volunteer, and thereby secure a place without the possibility of being removed and placed in the regular conscript army, was announced to be June 30.

Seymour, our neighboring town to the west, located in Webster County, was granted permission to organize a company of Missouri National Guards. The Supply Company of the new 6th Regiment of the National Guard of Missouri was comprised of volunteers from the Mansfield, Hartville, Ava, Seymour, Mountain Grove, and Cedar Gap areas. (The company was attached to the Army's 140th Infantry, 35th Division.) The Supply Company included Alva Carter, Garrett W. Carter, John A. Carter, Walter Coday, William Glenn Craig, Roy Handy, Frank D. Hoover, Clarence King, Roy Norcross, John Potts, Clyde Tarbutton, Claude E. Tripp, and Robert Viles, all from Mansfield; Franklin O. Briggs, William J. Roe, and John E. Spurlock of Ava; Howard Claxton and Robert Reed Whitteker of Hartville; Raymond Carrick, William W. Denny, Clifford L. Ferrell, and Ernest Packard of Seymour; and Lester E. Mingus of Cedar Gap. As this company was to oversee the wagon train of the regiment, the men were designated as cooks, wagoners (ones who drove the wagons), horseshoers, and munitions suppliers (ones who supplied troops at the front with ammunition and heavy artillery).

A series of fitness and medical tests followed their enlistment. Upon acceptance the men would experience months of basic training. Traversing these hills and hollers as they hunted for squirrels and raccoons most likely served them well in preparation for their fitness training.

Most of these young men had never left their families to journey outside these Ozark hills and had never traveled by ship or viewed the ocean.

Some members of the Supply Company from left to right (first row): Roy Handy, Howard Claxton, Roy Norcross, and Garrett William Carter; (second row) Claude Tripp, Alva Carter, Glenn Craig, Robert Viles, Clarence King, and Clyde Tarbutton; (third row) John Potts, R.R. Whitteker, Frank Hoover, and Walter Coday. "Mayor F. H. Riley presented the company a collie pup as a mascot, and the boys promptly named him Riley." (*Mansfield Mirror* Aug. 2, 1917)
(Courtesy of the MAHS Collection)

August 1917 brought about the departure of our boys to join their regiment; Mansfield hosted a farewell dinner in the flag-decorated city park. A large crowd of people gathered with basketfuls of good things to eat. "The Mansfield Bottling Works donated soda water and Fuson Drug Co. furnished ice cream. The Mansfield Drug offered cigars and P. W. Newton treated the honorees to anything they wanted in his store." (*Mansfield Mirror* Aug. 09, 1917)

Our troops preparing to board the train in Mansfield to travel to their training camps
(Courtesy of the MAHS Collection)

As a welcome distraction prior to the departure of the soldiers, some of them were able to participate in the Agricultural & Stock Show in Mansfield.

Mansfield's mayor, William G. Reynolds, served as President of the Agricultural and Stock Show. Fair premiums were $2.00 for 1st place in Horses and Mules, Cattle, Hogs, and Sheep/Goats. One of the main attractions was H. M. Norcross's 1,000-pound Poland China boar. Some familiar surnames that appeared as winners include Oetting, Gutschke, Fuge, P'Pool, Miller, Dennis, McCrite, Hoover, Martin, Rippee, and Craig.

(*Mansfield Mirror* Sept. 20, 1917)

As mentioned in the *Mansfield Mirror*, many area residents visited our boys at training camps, where they received both basic and specialized training in physical fitness, weapons proficiency, drill and discipline, field craft, trench warfare, cavalry tactics, machine gun operation, and artillery.

Allison Newton (R) wrote on the back of this card: This is the picture of me and a fellow
from near Mtn. Grove ready for action.
(Courtesy of the Kathy Short Collection)

"The boys of the Supply Company at Camp Clark in Nevada, Missouri were visited by several Mansfield citizens bringing them home-cooked goodies. By September Claude Tripp, Glenn Craig, and Roy Handy were detailed to guard the mule barns and the mules with Company I." (*Mansfield Mirror* Sept. 13, 1917)

Ernie Gaskill is shown with his sister Stella, who is visiting him at Camp Funston.
(Courtesy of the KS Collection)

Send Your Soldier Boy a Military Wrist Watch or a Fountain Pen, Something He Will Use Every Day.

(adv. Fuson Drug Company *Mansfield Mirror* Nov. 8, 1917)

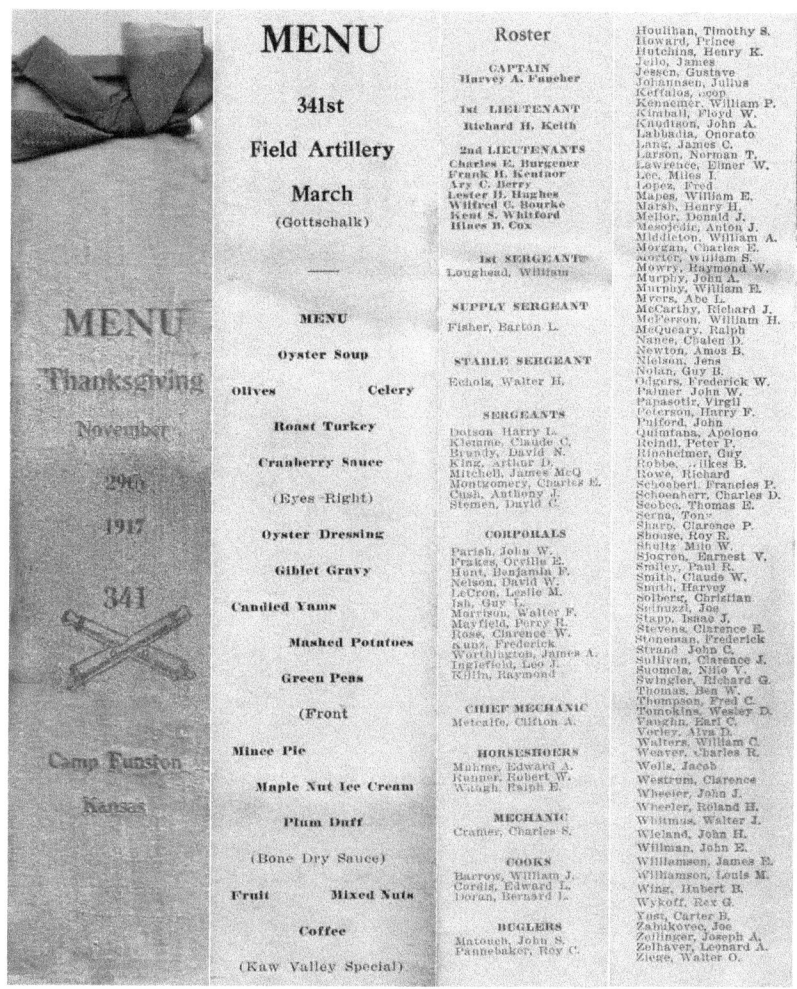

The pictures above depict the menu and the participants in the Thanksgiving dinner at Camp Funston for the 341st Field Artillery, held on November 29, 1917.

"Sunday is 'Food Saving Day' and requests have been sent out from Washington by Herbert Hoover that every minister preach Sunday upon the subject of Food Conservation."

(*Mansfield Mirror* June 28, 1917)

APRIL 1918 – NOVEMBER 1918

April 1918

Over There and Back Home

New York Harbor was one departure point for our troops.
(Public domain picture)

Although the time difference may have been seven hours, the soldiers spent approximately two weeks at sea before landing in France from America. By this time nearly a half million American soldiers had arrived in France. The Germans had advanced to Chateau-Thierry on the Marne River by late May.

Local servicemen headed out on their overseas journey filled their time swapping stories, playing cards, shooting craps, etc.

(Courtesy of the Henry Oscar Brown Collection.)

Over There:

Our area soldiers found themselves serving with the American Expeditionary Forces (A.E.F.), which was established in France in 1917 with Major General John J. "Black Jack" Pershing, a Missouri native, as its commander. They served with the Missouri National Guard and were later known as The Doughboys. The Salvation Army sent approximately 250 women volunteers armed with gas masks, helmets, and rolling pins to the Western Front. They fried up doughnuts to boost morale. "Today I made 22 pies, 300 doughnuts, and 700 cups of coffee," reported Margaret Sheldon (courtesy doughboy.org). These brave women became known as Doughnut Lassies or Dollies.

The Great War introduced a new form of warfare that used tanks, machine guns, and flame-throwers, but the most dangerous was the use of chemical warfare. The first use of chemical warfare in 1914 was by the French against Germany in the form of tear gas. In April 1915 at Ypres, the Germans used chlorine gas. The third agent used was Phosgene, which caused difficulty in breathing with an onset as much as 48 hours later. It is believed that Phosgene or a Phosgene/chlorine combination accounted for many deaths. Germans used mustard gas on the British forces at Ypres in 1917. Although it was not lethal, it caused chemical burns to skin, eyes, and respiratory tracts.

To counteract the effects of these various chemicals, soldiers were trained to use gas masks while they were on their missions.

Stereocards like this one were used in Stereoscopes for entertainment like the slides used in the View Masters from the 50s.

(Courtesy of the Ann Duckworth Collection)

Key Land Battles of the A.E.F.

"The soldiers of WWI were involved in the Battle of Chateau-Thierry, the Battle of Belleau Wood, the Battle of Saint-Mihiel which began September 12, 1918, and the Meuse-Argonne Offensive, which lasted from September 27 to October 6, 1918. The 110th Engineers served with the 35th Division and were thrown in the line in an emergency to help the infantry. They incurred heavy losses. They were ordered to cut barbed wire ahead of the advancing troops, concentrating on the roads crossing No Man's Land." (Courtesy of jstor.com)

During the battle in the Argonne Forest, it is known that the Engineers held off their attackers with their picks and shovels until the Infantry arrived.

E. E. Gaskill was one of the soldiers of the 35th Division that was assigned to cutting the barbed wire that impeded the advancement of our troops. This strip of land between the opposing trenches became a killing field. In relating his account of the battle, Gaskill told family members that he was the only one of his group who survived.

The War at Sea

German naval submarines, known as U-boats, were used to destroy merchant vessels carrying supplies to the Allied forces. Their ability to submerge and re-emerge surprised enemies and resulted in many casualties.

The *Lakemoor*, a steam-powered cargo carrier of 2,500 tons register, had recently been taken over by the shipping board. She was a new vessel that was sailing from an Atlantic port on her maiden trip. The *U.S.S. Lakemoor* was sunk by a German submarine, about midnight on April 11, 1918, in European waters.

"All the survivors have been tended at an English port. Out of a total of ten officers and fifty-two members of the crew, five officers and twelve of the crew have been reported as survivors. Among the survivors of the vessel is Clarence E. Hensley of Mansfield." (*Mansfield Mirror* April 25, 1918)

The Allies now began grouping their merchant ships into convoys with warship escorts for protection.

(Lake Moor (ID 218) located on the Naval History and Heritage Command website)

It took nearly one year after the Declaration of War to prepare our troops for battle. American soldiers were reluctant to say much of anything that was war-related for fear that their letters would never reach family back home. They were not permitted to reveal their exact location or any reference as to casualty reports. American troops did not enter the fighting in France until the spring of 1918, as referenced in the letter below.

Somewhere in France
April 21, 1918

Dear Mrs. S.W. McNaul,
My Dear Auntie,
Your letter received sometime back. How is everybody in Mansfield and the big boom? I suppose they are digging up all the hills; they are doing the same thing over here only with big shells; that is what takes all the joy out of the life. I got a nice big letter from Minnie, she seems to like it up in Washington fine. There is not much news here only war and we can't tell much about that through the mail. I suppose you read all about it in the papers. How is father coming? Rather lonely, I guess, since sister left home? I had a letter from Aunt Annie and Guy Taylor. Guy is some boy, would like to see him. Has Lovall Keeling come to France yet? He will find it all here. This sure is some fine country, but I don't like the climate much, too much rain to suit me.

I suppose Uncle has quit farming and gone to mining. From the rate Mansfield is going now I suppose it will be as large as New York City by the time I get back home. How do you like the meatless and wheatless days? That is the stuff to win the war, for food over here is very scarce. In some places money won't buy it. A loaf of bread cost 25 cents and eggs 75 cents a dozen and everything else is just as high. The only thing that is cheap is wine and you soon get filled up on that stuff. We don't get much coffee, mostly tea to drink. I guess it looks like springtime in old Missouri now. I think it will warm up here before long. Well, I don't have much news to tell. I am well and feeling fine.

Did they get Frank in the last draft, I haven't heard from him since I have been in France. Jess Ross is still here some place. I haven't seen him for quite a while but we expect to be back together soon. I must close for this time. Write me soon,

Your nephew,
Pvt. Harry B. Stephens

Pvt. Stephens referenced the rainy climate. Research shows that the wettest city in France in the month of April is Chatel, located in southeastern France, which could be a possible location for Stephens.

Back Home:

In January of 1918, to promote food conservation, the U.S. Food Administration was established and led by future president Herbert Hoover. Meatless Mondays and Wheatless Wednesdays permitted these goods to be exported to, not only our troops, but to the Allied nations where food was in short supply.

(Public domain picture)

U.S. Food Administration Poster
(Save meat and wheat for our Soldiers and Allies)
1) buy it with thought
2) cook it with care
3) use less wheat and meat
4) buy local foods
5) serve just enough
6) use what is left

Voluntary food rationing was adopted by all Americans. They were encouraged to substitute corn and oats for wheat and to use honey or syrup in place of sugar as sweeteners for the duration of the war.

"A telegram from the Washington Office of the Food Administration dated December 4th, says that the four pounds per month limitations for both public eating places and households have been removed." (*Mansfield Mirror* December 12, 1918)

Over There:

Manfred von Richthofen, known as the Red Baron, was born May 2, 1892, to a prominent family in what is now known as Poland. He began his military career in the cavalry, but trench warfare lacked the excitement he desired. He requested to be transferred to the German Air Service where he became a legendary ace fighter pilot. In his autobiography, *The Red Battle Flyer,* he credited his adversaries, "The Englishman is a smart fellow. That we must allow."

On April 21, 1918, near the Somme River in France, he came under fire by Australian machine gunners on the ground as well as a Canadian aircraft. It was unclear which rightfully could claim the victory. His death, clouded in mystery, and his prowess as an expert military aviator gave him celebrity status. Although only 25 years old, he was credited with having shot down 80 enemy aircraft. He has been immortalized in films, books, and songs including a pop composition in the 1960's.

Photo of the Red Baron's Fokker DRI on the ground (Public domain picture)

Back Home:

A major event in the Mansfield area centered around the growing interest in the mining industry. The *Kansas City Star* even sent a reporter to visit our area. Several prominent men from Nebraska, stockholders in the Pioneer Mining Company, were here looking over the mining situation.

Mr. Kendrick, boss of the Lead Hill Mine west of Mansfield, is shown supervising local residents Marion Lovall, Fred Morris, and John Davis.

(Courtesy of the KS Collection)

(Courtesy of the MAHS Collection)

The Nugget Theatre was showing the film *Who Goes There?* It was touted to be a great love story with a war background, and a noteworthy film adaptation from a novel by Robert W. Chambers.

Going to movies on Saturday afternoons often sparked lasting relationships. It was a fairly common practice for servicemen to marry before being shipped overseas. The term "war brides" originally referred to women who married their sweethearts who were leaving for military service. By the end of the Great War, the term "war brides" took on an entirely new meaning of international women marrying American soldiers serving overseas.

"Marvin H. Dennis, member of the Co. F, 110th Engineers, was wed to Miss Clella Gaskill at Fort Sill, Oklahoma. The bride returned to Mansfield to reside while her husband is fighting for Old Glory." (*Mansfield Mirror* April 11, 1918)

May 1918

Over There and Back Home

May 12, 1918

Dear parents and all,

I will write you all a few lines today to let you know I am still well and feeling fine. Well, I am over here at last in France; it sure is an odd country; everything is about 50 years behind time and it sure looks funny, too. The trains are small and still have spokes in the wheels, and nearly all the wagons are two wheeled carts yet with one horse to it.

Well, the weather is fine here at present, but it seems to rain pretty often; the gardens and such as that is ahead of any I saw back there when I left, so you see it is not so cold here as I have heard it was, but I guess it gets pretty cold through the winter though. I think I am going to like the country pretty good now.

Well, I hope you all are well yet but I guess it will be quite a while before I get to hear from you as they say the mail is slow coming this way and you need not worry if you don't hear from me for some time as the mail is apt to be delayed quite a bit at times and I don't think I'll get to write as often as I need to anyway but you can write just the same. But you will be sure to hear of it if anything is wrong. I don't think your mail will be censored, but all of mine will be so I can't tell you much about this country until I get home. But we are to have the best of treatment so there is nothing for you to worry about.

Well, it is a little further over here than I thought it was. I think there is about 7 hours difference in the time than there. Well, I guess I had better close before I write too much and get something in here that I should not.

So, I will close for this time with love to all,

Wm. Richard Schlicher
Co. B, 110th Engineers
American Expeditionary Forces

This French postcard shows a U.S. soldier posing next to a two-wheeled horsedrawn cart with four local children in it.

(From Folder 6, Early W. Smith Papers, WWI 42, Military Collection, State Archives of North Carolina, Raleigh, N.C., State Archives of North Carolina)

Treatment of German Americans and German Immigrants During the Great War

German immigrants had been arriving on American shores since the colonial period. Even in 1910, nine percent of our population had German heritage. Generally, Germans were regarded as hard-working, thrifty, and charitable and had integrated successfully into communities. When war broke out in Europe and news began to filter into America, divisions in the country began to emerge. Although many Americans wanted to stay out of the war, ones who wanted to fight, such as J.P. Morgan, were strongly aligned with the Allies. Some German Americans still felt a kinship to their fatherland and began to hold patriotic meetings, collect war relief funds for the Axis, and in some cases, even tried to return home to join the fight.

Once the United States declared war, anti-German sentiment resulted in a backlash against the German culture. Names of schools, foods, streets, towns, businesses, and even family names were changed to hide German ties. The German American family of John J. "Black Jack" Pershing had changed their name from Pfoerschin to Pershing when they first immigrated to America. Music by German composers was removed from concerts and homes. German businesses were vandalized; the German language, once a common part of the public-school curriculum was discontinued; German books were burned; and German newspapers were forced out of business. The dachshund was now called a liberty dog, and sauerkraut was given the name liberty cabbage.

Attacks were also made on individuals. Mansfield was no exception to the discrimination being felt by German immigrants and German Americans throughout the country. North of town in an area known as "Oetting Flats," a small German community had been formed by numerous German families. Oetting family folklore, shared with the authors, tells the story of "Grandpa" Oetting who decided to show his support of the old "Fatherland" and the Kaiser by attaching a German flag to the tailgate of his wagon and driving to Mansfield. When he arrived there, he was assaulted by a group of Mansfield citizens who supported the Allies and was told not to show his flag again in Mansfield. The next day he once again drove his wagon to town with the attached flag and was beaten again.

The Espionage Act of 1917 granted the Postmaster General the power to censor mail. It was passed prior to the embarkment of our troops and allowed the government to spy on the correspondence of German Americans. After our soldiers entered the war, this act had a huge effect on what they would communicate to their families. Any information regarding unit location was forbidden, as well as anything that could be perceived as damaging to morale. In WWI, war correspondents were also censored except for the A.E.F. In France under General Pershing's command, they were permitted to go to the front lines without a military escort. Many soldiers chose to self-censor their letters and often downplayed the dangers that they were facing so as not to alarm the family back home.

Somewhere in France

Dear Parents and all,

I will write you a few lines today to let you know I am still well and feeling fine, and hope you are all the same. I guess you have begun to think that I have quit writing but there is so little that I can write that I never write very often, but I will try to write you a little as often as I can, but that will not be very often. But you need not worry for you will be sure to hear it if I get sick or hurt.

We are in a nice place now, but I don't know how long we will stay here for they move us about quite a bit so we get to see quite a lot of the country. I am just about out of anything to write. I have not got any mail for a few days now so I guess I will get several letters when I do get my mail again.

You had better write about that allotment again if you are not getting it yet for you should get it every month now.

I will close for this time, with love to all,

Wm. Richard Schlicher

Co. B, 110th Engineers

American Expeditionary Forces

As referenced in the previous letter, soldiers often had allotments taken from their paychecks and mailed to their families back home to provide financial support during their absence.

Form 317

TREASURY DEPARTMENT
BUREAU OF WAR RISK INSURANCE
MILITARY AND NAVAL DIVISION

This Bureau has received from the enlisted man named on the other side of this card a statement showing that he has made an allotment of a part of his pay to you

Action with a view to making payment will be taken as soon as possible, but it may be thirty days before you receive notice of final action. If you should find it necessary to write to this Bureau, give the enlisted man's name and organization and the number as stated on this card.

BUREAU OF WAR RISK INSURANCE.

TREASURY DEPARTMENT
BUREAU OF WAR RISK INSURANCE
OFFICIAL BUSINESS
RETURN AFTER FIVE DAYS

PENALTY FOR PRIVATE USE $300

Number
S-3796370

Enlisted Man
Willis H. Mitchell

Organization
Bat 22-164 DB
Cp. Funston,
Kan

Ruby M. Mitchell
R.F.D. #1
Ava.
Mo

(Courtesy of the Kay Dunnegan Goss Collection)

The deduction for the soldier's War Risk Insurance is shown on the payment book. This was a military life insurance, which would be awarded to the family in the event of the soldier's death.

(Courtesy of the KDG Collection)

Back Home:

Son Is Missing

"Mrs. Leona Akers, who resides fifteen miles south of Norwood has received official notice from the War Department at Washington that her son, Walter Akers, is listed among those reported as missing at the close of the day's action on the eastern front on April 14th. Young Akers was among the first from this part of the country to volunteer after the United States declared war and he has been in active service in France since last fall. Mrs. Akers also has another son, H. J. Akers, in France, who volunteered early in the war. He is serving with the marine corps." *(Mansfield Mirror May 16, 1918, as reprinted from the Springfield Republican)*

Camp Funston, located on Fort Riley near Manhattan, Kansas, provided training classes in hippology. All farriers were trained in hippology, which was the study of horses. Their duties were to keep horses and mules shod and hooves trimmed. These troops were also trained in equine disease prevention, so they could assist the veterinarians. The stable sergeants' responsibilities included stable care and organization of the picket line. The picket lines were carefully maintained as the soldier's horse and equipment had to be readily accessible. The picket line was used to tether the equine soldiers at night, making them vulnerable to poisonous gas attacks. Furthermore, severe foot problems often resulted from them having to stand in a mixture of mud and excrement. Although combat deaths were not frequent, thousands of horses were treated daily for bullet wounds, gas, and even shell shock. The loss of a horse was sometimes more of an issue than the loss of a soldier because there were no replacements to be found for horses.

These two pictures show some of the members of the Department of Hippology M.S.S. Horseshoers and Stable Sgts. Classes in Fort Riley, Kansas, May 19, 1918.

(Courtesy of the HS Collection)

June 1918

Over There and Back Home

June 26, 1918

Hello, Sis,

Thought I had better write you a few lines before you snatch me bald headed. Well, how are you? This leaves me feeling fine. Suppose you are having some time now raising good things to eat, also little chicks. Gee, how I would like to have a chick's hind leg!

29

Nothing much to write, haven't received any mail from home since leaving New York. Got a letter from Stella yesterday dated May 23, so it was on the road about a month.

I like the country fine here-just like living on a farm, hear the roosters crow and the birds singing and everything that makes life more like home. There are even horses and cows at the same place, so you can imagine I am not homesick. Didn't get seasick while on the water, only a few of the boys did. Lots of seed stuff grown here, such as lettuce, onions, mustard, cabbage, beans and nearly any kind of a flower you can name-some of the prettiest flower gardens you ever saw. Haven't learned to talk French yet, so I am out of luck with the girls. Hardly ever see a boy who looks like he is over 15 or 16.

Am out in a park, as we would call it now; a fine place to write, nice and cool. Everything looks odd here, even the town; the buildings are so low, and crooked and narrow streets. Would have room in our streets to put a block of their town, that's one thing that makes it look odd.

As news is scarce I will close for now and wait for mail. Answer soon and send all the news you can. Tell all hello. Don't forget me while I am gone.

With love to all,
Pvt. Clifford M. Seal
Hdqrs. Co., 129th Field Artillery,
A.P.O. 733
American E. F., via New York

Letters began to arrive home describing the European countryside. Some of the troops would include pictures inside these letters.

When soldiers ventured into local towns, citizens would often to come out to observe their activities.

Street scene circa 1918 (Courtesy of the HS Collection)

Some of the soldiers learned enough French that they were able to socialize with the young women in the area.

Picture of European ladies
(Courtesy of the HS Collection)

Soldier Bob Davis recounted the story of the time he was separated from his unit. He arrived at a French farm, weary and hungry. The family allowed him to hide under the hay in their barn. He did not know the French language, so when he saw a chicken, he mimicked one, flapping his arms and acting as if he were cracking eggs. The women understood and made him a meal of three eggs. He eventually learned some of the language from this family.

July 1918

Over There and Back Home

July 2, 1918

Home Folks,

Your letter received last night that was written June 1, was sure glad to hear from all and to know all were well. I am fine. I have moved from where I was at the last letter I wrote you. We started out one evening and camped at a small town that night and the next day we made it to our stopping place. Don't know how long we will be here but it is not as close to the firing line as we were. Some of the boys in my company has been up to the trenches and the shells fell close enough to them that it threw dirt in their wagons, but I have not been up yet.

I bought a postcard book of the different towns that I have been in and had the clerk mail them back to you, one to Anna. I could not send them but he claimed he could, so if you get it, you can tell where I have been.

I am now near the heavy artillery firing, but it is quite a-ways from the place we left last. They shot several shells over us on the railroad blowing the railing in two as if they were twine strings.

Well, you wanted to know if we had plenty to eat -- yes, when we are in camp, but when we are on the road we do not have so much, I haven't gone hungry very long at a time.

The Red Cross sales must be taking in quite a bit. Anna wrote and said a rooster sold for over $200 at Mt Grove. I would like to see that quilt father gave $51 for.

I saw the Mansfield Mirror this morning but they were old. April and May. I am glad to hear the crops are good for we may need some over here.

Tell all hello, for I will close for this time.

Goodbye.

Claude Tripp

Claude Tripp in uniform
(Courtesy of the KS Collection)

Two postcards from an overseas accordion
postcard book

Back Home:

"Miss Harriett Oberholser passed military examination before Dr. R. M. Rogers preparatory to doing Red Cross work in France." (*Mansfield Mirror* July 4, 1918)

The American Red Cross was formed to serve as a medium of communication between the troops in the field and their families at home. Local Red Cross chapters held fundraising auctions that were well-attended.

Red Cross

Red Cross Auction
Public Square, Mansfield, Mo.
Saturday, May 4, 1918

"A great net of mercy drawn through an ocean of unspeakable pain"

"I'm afraid that's all I can spare"

You're a regular, red-blooded, true-blue American. You love your country. You love that flapping, snapping old flag; your heart thumps hard when the troops tramp by. You're loyal--100 per cent!

You intend to--you want to--help win the war in a hurry.

"Sacrifice? Sure," you've been thinking. "Just you wait till they really need it." And you've honestly thought that too.

But--look yourself in the eye, now, and search up and down inside of your heart---did you mean it? Did you really mean "sacrifice?"

Listen: You feel poor. This Third Liberty Loan, the high prices, the Income Tax---you've done your bit. You feel that you've given all you can spare.

What? Then what did you mean? What's that we said about loving your county? What did you think the word "sacrifce" means?

Surely you didn't mean, did you, to give only what you can spare?

What about our boys who are giving their lives in the trenches? Are they giving only what they can "spare?"

How about those mothers and little "kiddies" in the shell--wrecked towns of that war-swept hell:-- hungry--ragged--sobbing--alone? Give up their homes, their husbands, their fathers.

While we, over here with our fun and comforts, we hold up our heads and feel patriotic because we have given--what? Some loose bills off the top of our roll. "We've given all we can spare!"

Come, Come! Let's quit fooling ourselves. Let us learn what "sacrifice" means. Let us give more than we can spare. Let us "give till the heart says stop."

(*Mansfield Mirror*)

"Sheriff C. G. Sanders of Hartville was here Monday. He recently made an arrest near Macomb of a deserter from Camp Dodge, Iowa and took him to Ft. Leavenworth, Kas." (*Mansfield Mirror* July 18, 1918)

"Mansfield's Masonic Lodge provided the Red Cross ladies with a convenient work room. Included in their first overseas shipment were twelve dozen handkerchiefs, two dozen wash rags, 20 pairs of socks, and 2 packages of triangular bandages as they reportedly were hindered by a shortage of supplies." (*Mansfield Mirror* July 18, 1918)

Later shipments would include bed shirts, undergarments, trench foot socks, and helpless case shirts made per Red Cross specifications.

These helpless case shirts were to be sewn from a length of 47" of light cotton fabric, open down the front, having only side seams and three string ties. These garments were designed for men who suffered catastrophic war injuries.

Over There:

July 3, 1918

Dear Father and Mother,

I will drop you a few lines today. This leaves me well and enjoying myself fine.

We took a hike the other day of 32 miles, the longest that has been taken by American troops in France. We were on the Amiens front for a while but have left there now. There is where we saw the German aeroplane fall. There was two men in it and they were burnt pretty badly, they dropped shells in about 100 yards of us but didn't frighten us any.

I want you to send me some tobacco and candy. They issue some Durham.

Is Virgil at home? Tell him to write and you write more often; I received your letter of June 10. I write often when we get settled, paper is hard to get here and we haven't been around a YMCA. Hoping to hear from you soon.

Your son,

Ralph Dake

Co. F, 110 Engineers

Soldiers would often ask their families to send them specific items, such as tobacco, candy, and patent medicines (over-the-counter medicines).

Polar Bear Expedition

On July 17, 1918, President Woodrow Wilson established the Murmansk Expedition, which was formed from American forces selected by General Pershing on July 30, 1918. The Americans belonging to the expedition, which was later dubbed the Polar Bear Expedition, were sent to Siberia. These men were assigned to guard duty along the railway to protect the large amounts of military supplies in the Archangel-Murmansk area from Communist forces.

The troops served under miserable conditions due to the extreme temperatures. Horses were not equipped to handle the sub-zero temperatures of Russia, and neither were some of the munitions. During the ensuing months, many soldiers continued to fight in Russia well past the signing of the Armistice and suffered approximately 200 casualties. Many men died from multiple causes due to problems with fuel, ammunitions, supplies, and food availability.

The Murmansk Expedition was redesignated as the American North Russia Expeditionary Forces on September 12, 1918, and as the A.E.F., North Russia on April 9, 1919. The expedition was discontinued upon withdrawal of the last American military units on August 5, 1919.

Born and raised in the Lead Hill community between Mansfield and Cedar Gap, James A. Morris was one of the brave soldiers who served with the Polar Bear Expedition from 1918 to 1919 in the Co. F, 31st Infantry. The following pictures are postcards sent to his brother John Morris of Cedar Gap.

James A. Morris
in uniform

The ship that was iced over
when they arrived at
Vladivostok, Russia, 1918

Some of Morris's Russian
buddies

(Courtesy of the KS Collection)

James Morris in Russia after his release from the hospital

Back Home:

"Marvin H. Dennis, a member of Co. F, 110th Engineers, now with the American Expeditionary Forces, somewhere in France; has sent to his parents, Joe H. Dennis and wife, of Mansfield, a part of a German plane, which fell near him, killing the two German aviators. The plane was brought down by the British forces, and the engine of the plane was still running when it struck the ground." (*Mansfield Mirror* July 18, 1918)

Photo of a captured German Fokker during WWI (Public domain picture)

Prisoners of War

"A Washington dispatch from the War Department announces that the American minister at Berne stated that Lieut. L. M. Edens of Cabool had been transferred from the German prison camp Karlsruhe to a camp at Villingen. Walter Akers of Norwood is at the prison camp at Darmstadt." (*Mansfield Mirror* July 18, 1918)

The prison camp, Karlsruhe, lies east of the Rhine River along the northern edge of the Black Forest. Villingen is located on the eastern edge of the Black Forest, while Darmstadt is located on the Upper Rhine Plain, between Basel and Frankfurt, Germany.

A photo circa 1900 of the Karlsruhe German prison camp in which Lieut. L. M. Edens was held at one point (Public domain picture)

A 1915 photo of the Darmstadt prison camp in which Walter Akers was held

(Retrieved from the Digital Public Library of America https://scholarworks.wmich.edu/wwi_pow_camps/917)

"Snippets from Home"

"Herve E. Coday, who had been attending the Springfield Business College, left last week for St. Louis to join the navy. He failed to pass the [physical] examination and returned home." (*Mansfield Mirror* July 25, 1918)

Incidentally, it was reported that approximately ¼ of the WWI draftees were rejected for various reasons. "In Wright County, there were 60 men certified and 93 not certified." (*Mansfield Mirror* Aug. 30, 1917)

"William R. Greenwood departed for Indianola, Warren County, Iowa, Sunday evening where he reports for army service Wednesday; he has been doing his "bit" this summer by farming, having a very large crop and stock. Of course, we will all miss him from our circle; but we do not suppose he will miss us as he was anxious to go; his will be the first star in the service flag for Macomb Sunday School and the first for the Christian Endeavor, but more to follow soon. We wish him success, happiness, good service for his country, and a safe return home." (*Mansfield Mirror* July 25, 1918)

Fighting Intensifies

July 25, 1918

Somewhere in France

Home Folks,

Hello to all. How are all at home? I am fine and dandy. Guess you will think I am dead by the time you get this, but I am not. We haven't had any outgoing mail service for a few days.

I am now under shellfire and have been for some time, but I do not mind that. I got three letters from you and four from Anna and one from Marvin Dennis, all at the same time. And the same night I got Marvin's letter I saw him, he is close here where I am now; so are Ernest Gaskill and Sherman Borders, but I haven't got to see them yet.

How are the sick folks back there? So Aunt Betty is sick? I haven't seen Clyde for about a week or more. He is not with me at present. I'm glad corn is looking as good as it is. You say Walter Coday wrote home that he had been within 25 miles of the firing line, I have got that beat. I have been within 100 yards of the trenches, and shells whistling through the air.

Tell Father I have got that dime yet. Have you ever got that postcard book that I sent some time ago, and my insurance papers I sent back? I guess I have written about all I can for this time. Tell all hello for me. I will close before I write something that I ought not to. I will write again soon. I close, hoping to see you all before another year.

Goodbye,

Claude E. Tripp

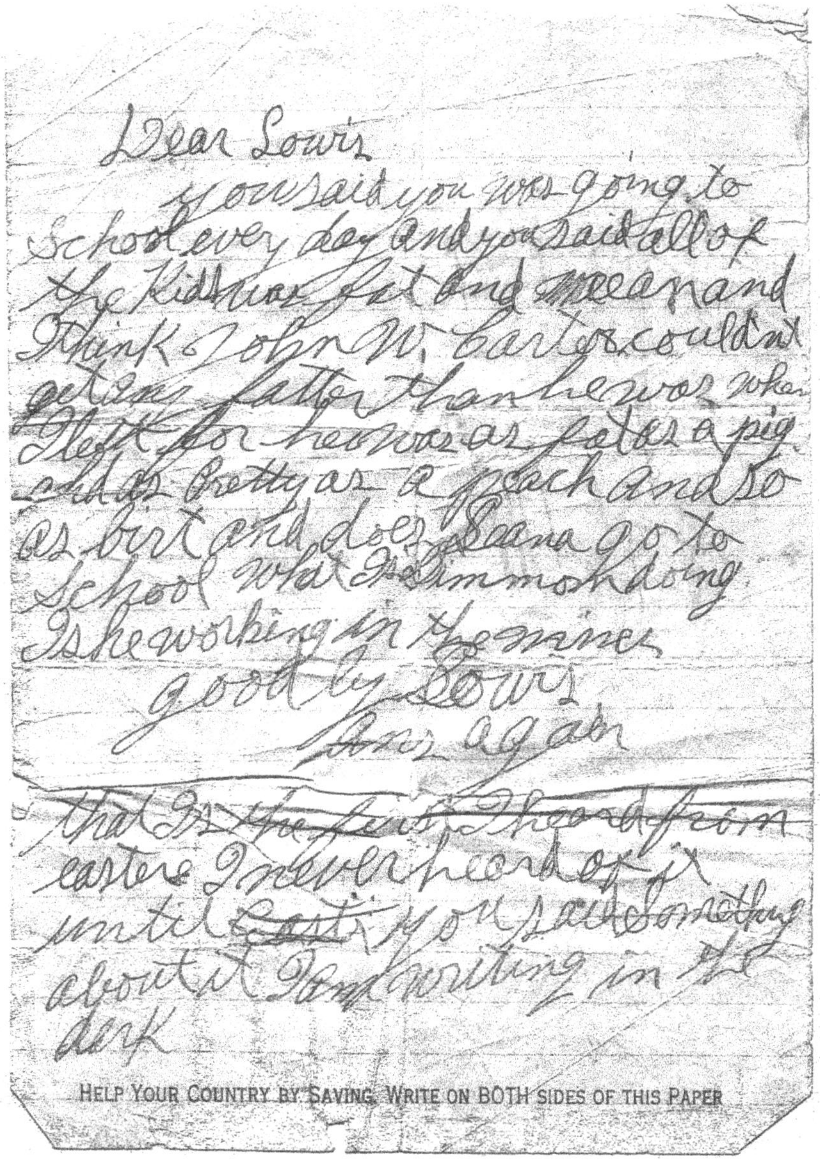

Dear Lowis

You said you was going to school every day and you said all of the kids was fat and mean and I think John W. Carter couldn't get any fatter than he was when I left for he was as fat as a pig and as pretty as a peach and so as Bert and does Sana go to school What is Simmon doing Is he working in the mines

good by Lowis
ans again

that is the first I heard from Carter I never heard of it until you said something about it I am writing in the dark

HELP YOUR COUNTRY BY SAVING. WRITE ON BOTH SIDES OF THIS PAPER

The letter above is difficult to read as it was written by Mansfield native Clarence King as he struggled to see in the darkness of the trenches.

(Courtesy of the King family)

While Ernie Gaskill was in a hospital recovering from mustard gas, he carved insignias into a munition shell, now known as trench art.

(Courtesy of the KS Collection)

The Sanitary Corps collected the used cartridge shells and recycled some of them to the hospitals to serve as rehabilitation therapy for the soldiers.

Realities of War

July 28, 1918
Somewhere

To Col. Roy Dennis,

How are crops? They are OK here. About all they have where we are now is grass and plenty of good drinking water. You can see three different countries from here, but there is one I long to see – looks like I might, some day or other.

We worked a week ago Saturday and then walked about 8 miles that night with a pack, I took a bath about a couple of months ago in the Atlantic or English Channel but could not quite swim across. It sure is some salty, too.

How are your colts? Be back when we get the kaiser, and not before.

Marvin Dennis

Our soldiers were forbidden to give their location; however, there is a site in France that two more countries are visible, that being Germany and Switzerland.

In the past, auctioneers were required to have a valid real estate license. After they qualified for the job, some auctioneers took the title of colonel. This practice dated back to the Civil War when only military colonels were allowed to auction off the spoils of war. In the salutation of this letter, Col. refers to the fact that Roy Dennis was an auctioneer.

In this picture, the patriarch of the Dennis family, Joseph Harrison Dennis, is featured on the left beside his sons Marvin (Marve), Ural, Roy, Dwight, and A. B. (Bill) Dennis, circa 1918. Mr. Dennis had given each of his sons a foal out of his favorite mare. Here, they pose with the mare and her offspring on the square during the Mansfield Carnival and Stock Show.

(Courtesy of Larry Dennis)

July 28, 1918

U.S.S. New Mexico

Dear Friends,

I left the Great Lakes the evening of the 11th about 3 o'clock. We traveled out across the plains of Illinois. We traveled all of that night and hit the mountains early the next morning. We traveled down the Ohio could see the beautiful mountain scenery of Kentucky and Ohio. We traveled through Kentucky almost all day and then crossed over to W.Va., the mountains getting higher all the time. About all you could see was a big coal chute running from the top down to a car on the sidetrack. Then we went out of W.Va. and went through a tunnel 1½ miles long; then we hit the Blue Ridge mountains of Va., it was about sunset when we hit them. There were some pretty pictures –the sun shining out across the valleys.

Our first stop in Va. was at White Sulphur Springs. The people took us out and showed us the summer resorts. They sure was some fine marble buildings, surrounded by big, tall pines; then we started on the journey again. We didn't stop anymore until we reached New Port News. There we got on a boat and sailed across the Chesapeake Bay to Norfolk Va. I was at Norfolk a week then I took the ship for my present destination. I got to sail about 350 miles on the ocean for my first trip.

I have written about all that I am allowed to write, so I will close.

Yours truly,
Earl R. Gilley
U.S.S. New Mexico
P.M.N.Y. City

July 28, 1918
Somewhere

To Joe H. Dennis,

Boo, boo! Freezing off this morning; cold as Christmas up here; rains nearly every day. We are digging trenches; don't look like they would ever use them. We are up in the mountains, about 3,500 feet above sea level; wind blows pretty cold; doesn't seem like summer is as near over as it is.

Guess you are done haying by now. I saw some of the Mansfield boys; they stay near us. Looks like the *Boches were about licked; hope so, anyway. We're not in the country we landed in. One good thing about this country is that we have plenty of good water. We've moved once since I wrote you –think we will move again in about two weeks.

The last Mirror I received was May 30; ought to have some mail in a few days. Well, tell me the news; give me the addresses of the boys that have left.

Marvin Dennis

*The French word "boches" was a derogatory expression used to indicate German soldiers.

After a bombing mission over German lines, circa 1918, this aerial photograph was taken from an American airplane of the French Air Service Breguet biplane returning from this mission.
(Public domain picture)

These postcards of German officers were brought home by servicemen as souvenirs.
(Courtesy of the MAHS Collection)

The postcard on the left depicts "Kaiser Bill" or Kaiser Wilhelm II, Emperor of Germany and King of Prussia, who was forced to abdicate and live in exile in the Netherlands following Germany's defeat at the hands of the Allied nations of France, Britain, Russia, Italy, and the United States.

The postcard on the right depicts German General Paul Von Hindenburg. The Hindenburg line, the last German defensive barrier, was breached in October 1918. The American Expeditionary Forces, under the command of General John J. Pershing, penetrated this line during what has come to be known as the Meuse-Argonne Offensive. The combined efforts of the Allied Nations using artillery, tanks, and aircraft resulted in Germany's retreat and eventual defeat and surrender.

July 30, 1918
Somewhere in France

Dear Ones at Home,

I received two letters from you today and was sure glad to hear again. I am well and getting along fine, but can't say I like this country. I like England fine, but I can't get anything out of this language and they are about 100 years behind the times here. They work bulls by the horns, and mules with a yoke. I haven't seen a set of harness or a four wheel wagon since I've been here. I have seen four sawmills here. But they don't know how to saw. I never saw a mill like these; only they have a Jack Wilson set of workers.

Well, tell Uncle Gordon he can run old Casey this year, but I think I will next. If things don't make an awful big change, I'll take Christmas dinner at home. I hope so anyway.

The *Sammies have gained awful fast and still at it. You tell Ernie Crippen that I said he ought to be glad he didn't get in the Navy for the dark blue is awful deep and rough; when the waves hit the smokestack it seems pretty lonesome. I was sick three days and nights at first, and there are other things to make you sick at sea, but I am safe on land again and only 4,750 miles from home.

I guess Papa is thrashing yet. I'm sure glad to hear your crops look so good. I will close, hoping to hear from you soon.

With love to all,
Ira Stout

*The term *Sammies* referred to Uncle Sam's troops.

(Public domain picture)

The origin of Uncle Sam dates to the War of 1812. He is portrayed as an older bearded man dressed in clothes that evoke the U.S. Flag. The "I Want You" recruitment poster by James Montgomery Flagg was distributed to encourage enlistment in the army. Even though the image of Uncle Sam had been used since the War of 1812, the poster solidified the image as a patriotic figure and became synonymous with patriotic duty. Uncle Sam is the Spirit of America. The patriotic hero will live as long as America will.

July 30, 1918

Camp Pike, Ark.

Dear Friends and Readers of the Mirror,

I will try to write a few lines for I would be lost without the paper. I had a good time coming down. We had some time at Mountain Grove. One of our men fell off the train; so we got in 5 miles of Cabool. The conductor said, "He can come on the next train," but we went back, met him, and came on to Cabool. Our next stop was West Plains-not much there – and then Thayer. We made it to Arkansas and the road wasn't straight all the way. We stopped in Newport for about an hour and saw 10,000 acres of cotton. There were frogs on the tracks. We stopped again at Little Rock then on to Camp Pike, and I am here.

I have been doing nothing for a week but eat. I feel 100% better. I am 12 or 14 pounds heavier than I was. Uncle Sam feeds us well. I have eaten beef and spuds till I do not want to look at them. I am up at the YMCA. I may be gone by the time you get this letter. This camp has 120,000 soldiers and is 8 miles square.

One of my Wright County friends went over to take out his insurance – and after he signed up for $10,000 a big auto truck ran over him and broke his leg in 3 places – it sure was too bad. Lieut. Clifton Robinett is two miles from me and I am in speaking distance of Geo. Gaskill.

Yours truly,
Joe H. Smith

August 1918

Over There and Back Home

Back Home:

"Snippets from Home"
"The Mansfield Bottling Works is temporarily out of business because of an inability to secure a supply of sugar." (*Mansfield Mirror* Aug 1, 1918)

(Courtesy of the MAHS Collection)

The Mansfield Bottling Works was at one time owned by the Brasher family. It was located across the tracks, south of the public square. In 1912, the company began bottling Orcherade, soon followed by Orange Crush and Grapette sodas. Shipments were made nationwide by rail.

In spite of the hot, dry weather, schools were preparing to commence classes, and the primary election was gearing up. Candidates for Wright County Recorder of Deeds were Barney Yates, A. F. Richardson, and Charley Hensley, all of Hartville, as well as Robert Morton of Macomb and Guy Newton of Manes, all Republicans. Community singings were also well attended. (*Mansfield Mirror* August 1, 1918)

Preparations were being made for Mansfield's seventh annual Agriculture and Stock Show. Changes in the festivities were to include one day to be set aside as Patriotic Day, and premiums were to be paid by Thrift Stamps. Mrs. A. J. Wilder was to be the Superintendent of the Poultry Department.

"Wright County's Salvation Army quota of $1,000.00 had not yet been met and Pleasant Valley Township was still $31.50 away from their quota." (*Mansfield Mirror* August 8, 1918)

"Organizations and Sunday Schools recognized our local soldiers by placing a star on their Service Flag. The Masons had Clifton Robinett, Jesse Roote, Walter Coday, Carlyle Poe, Frank Pope, Edward Whitwer, Oscar Renn, Hina Maberry, Ernest J. Butzke, Harry Hays, and Harold Livingston. Cumberland Presbyterian Service Flag represents: Walter Coday, Alva Carter, Garrett Carter, Frank Ross, Jess Ross, Walter Beach,

Verner Rippee, John Potts, Karl Tripp, Elmer Strong, Charlie Brentlinger, Paul Younger, Clarence King, Elbert King, Herbert Short, Charley James, and Dee Gaskill. Methodist Church Service Flag contains eight stars for Frank Hoover, Cecil Hoover, Ed. Westbrook, Harry Mooney, Clelland Hitchcock, Glenn Craig, and Ira Young and Raymond Young." (*Mansfield Mirror* Aug 15, 1918)

The Spanish Flu epidemic created shortages of nurses, hospital beds, coffins, morticians, and doctors.

Medical Classifications

"Dr. R. M. Rogers, Chairman of the Council of Medical Defense, has been ordered to see every physician in Wright and Douglas counties by August 20th for classification. All doctors are classified as follows: Class I: those already commissioned in the Medical Reserve Corps., Class II: those under 55 years of age, Class III: those over 55 years of age. He does not expect to find a slacker physician in either county; if he finds a slacker, his name will be given later." (*Mansfield Mirror* August 15, 1918)

"Dr. R. M. Rogers, Chairman of the Council of Medical Defense reports the following classifications:

Class I: Dr. E. C. Witwer, Mountain Grove; Dr. H. G. Frame, Mountain Grove; Dr. J. D. Ferguson, Ava.

Class II: Drs. R. A. Ryan and L. T. Van Noy of Norwood; Drs. A. J. Farmer and B. E. Latimer of Hartville; Dr. A. C. Ames of Mountain Grove; Dr. J. R. Mott of Grovespring; Dr. J. A. Fuson of Mansfield.

Class III: Dr. R. M. Norman of Ava; Drs. J. M. Hubbard and H. U. Daugherty and Chas. Palmer of Mountain Grove; Dr. J R. Davis of Noble; Dr. C. L. Wilson of Hartville; Drs. Wm. M. Hamilton and R. M. Rogers of Mansfield." (*Mansfield Mirror* August 22, 1918)

"Snippets from Home"

"Karl Tripp's address is now Headquarters' Company, 70th Infantry, Camp Funston, Kansas, he having become a member of the Army band. He was a member of the famous Mansfield Concert Band before entering the Army." (*Mansfield Mirror* Aug. 22, 1918)

Military bands provided a distraction and were a boost to morale. They performed in dress parades and ceremonies and provided entertainment at hospitals. Some prominent American military musicians were Irving Berlin and John Philip Sousa.

"The Woman's Council of Defense is assisting the Red Cross in securing nurses for the hospital services at home and abroad. Wright County's quota is 10. Women between the ages of 19 and 35 are eligible - must have at least two years in high school and be of good moral character and in good health." (*Mansfield Mirror* Aug 29, 1918)

Over There:

A mere fifteen years after the Wright brothers flew their plane at Kitty Hawk, air warfare was introduced. The Battle of Amiens, along the Somme River in northwestern France, launched on August 8, 1918, was a major turning point in the war. Combined air, artillery, infantry, and tanks moved to the front under cover of darkness and caught the Germans by surprise. General Erich von Ludendorff, the German Commander in Chief, referred to this as the "Black Day of the German Army." It was reported that the Germans lost more ground on this date than any other on the Western Front. This offensive sparked the Hundred Day Campaign.

Tanks, also known as "land ships," were developed to break the stalemate of the trench warfare along the Western Front. The first battle in which the American Expeditionary Forces used tanks that were operated by Americans was in September 1918. The version they used was the Renault FT tank designed by the French. This tank was lighter and faster than the heavy British models then being used and was manufactured in large quantities. The FT could reach top speeds of 6 mph and were manned by only two men. These armored, all-terrain vehicles assisted the infantry across the barbed wire, craters, and trenches. Although the United States did manufacture tanks, none of them saw combat duty in WWI.

Soldiers posing on one of the Renault FT tanks
(Courtesy of the HS Collection)

August 23, 1918

Somewhere in France

Dear Sister,

Will try to answer your most welcome letter that I received last night; our letters are scarce over here now. I received a nice, long letter from mother yesterday also, and I was sure glad to get it. I try to write her at least once a week, but I have been so busy lately that I can't find time to write.

Last night there was a German airplane come down close enough to the ground that you could have hit him with a rock and he turned a machine gun loose on the billets where some of our company was and believe me there was some dodging took place. One shell came through the roof and on through the bed of our mess sergeant, but he wasn't in the bed. They all thought it was a French plane until he turned his machine gun loose and then it was too late to shoot at him and he got away. All day today the Germans have been trying to get back over our lines, but all have failed.

We got paid Sunday and on Monday there were four of us ate 24 eggs, a gallon of potatoes, a bottle of pickles, and 3 cans of jam. Take it from me, I was sure full for once, but we get fairly good eats and haven't any room to complain, but you know a fella wants a little something extra every once in a while.

You asked me to write and tell you what I was doing and all about my work. Well, I have 132 head of horses and mules and 32 men here and the rest of the stock and the rest of the men are working just back of the trenches, taking supplies to the men in the trenches and we are about three miles back from them. I would like to go into details and tell you all about it but I am afraid it wouldn't go through, but this will give you an idea of what I have to do and how we handle the supplies. We have lost quite a few men out of our regiment but not as many as one would think for.

Well, I guess I will have to close for this letter is for all of you. So answer by return mail.

With love to all, your brother,

Frank D. Hoover

Time in the trenches was treacherous. Troops would spend a few days on the front line, followed by a period of rest when they were given hot meals and letters from home.

Farriers

Farriers, or smiths, as they were also known, were the war horses' first line of defense. They were usually non-commissioned officers serving with artillery or cavalry units. They were blacksmiths with some equine physiology knowledge as well.

Farriers' duties were varied, whereas those of the saddlers, horseshoers, and wagoners were more specific. Saddlers were in charge of cleaning and repairing all leather equipment such as reins, harnesses, collars, and hames. Horseshoers' backbreaking duty of shoeing was also accompanied by general hoof care, as they were to inspect the feet of the equine soldiers two times daily. The wagoner was responsible for his team, harness, wagon, and tools and parts needed for wagon and harness repairs. However, the farriers' duties as described in the *Manual for Farriers, Horseshoers, Saddlers, and Wagoners* document #486, issued by the War Department in 1917, laid out their responsibilities to include treating and disinfecting wounds and injuries, as well as administer medications, treat colic, lameness, mange, eczema, lice, and worms." (*Digital Public Library of America*)

Men in the trenches in a photo taken by a local soldier. (Courtesy of the HS Collection)

Due to the extremely muddy conditions, it could take 12 hours per day to clean and inspect the horses and to clean their harnesses. Pine tar was a sticky antiseptic substance that was used in dressings to promote healing. The farriers used the pine tar in salves for cuts, burns, and other injuries.

It appears that the legs of the horse in this picture are being treated with pine tar. (Courtesy of the HS Collection)

Farriers, as well as their horses, were expected to march as much as 40 miles per day, carrying heavy loads. These men were also delegated the task of humane disposal of their wounded or sick horses. Oft times, the hungry animals would chew through their gas masks, mistaking them for feed bags. Death and destruction at the hands of enemy snipers, trained to aim at the animals' lower legs, were imminent. Countless horses and mules were euthanized to end their suffering. (Prior to the U. S. involvement in the war, Missouri held the contract with the British Army and supplied more than 350,000 mules. Consequently, Lathrop, Missouri became known as the Mule Capital of the World.)

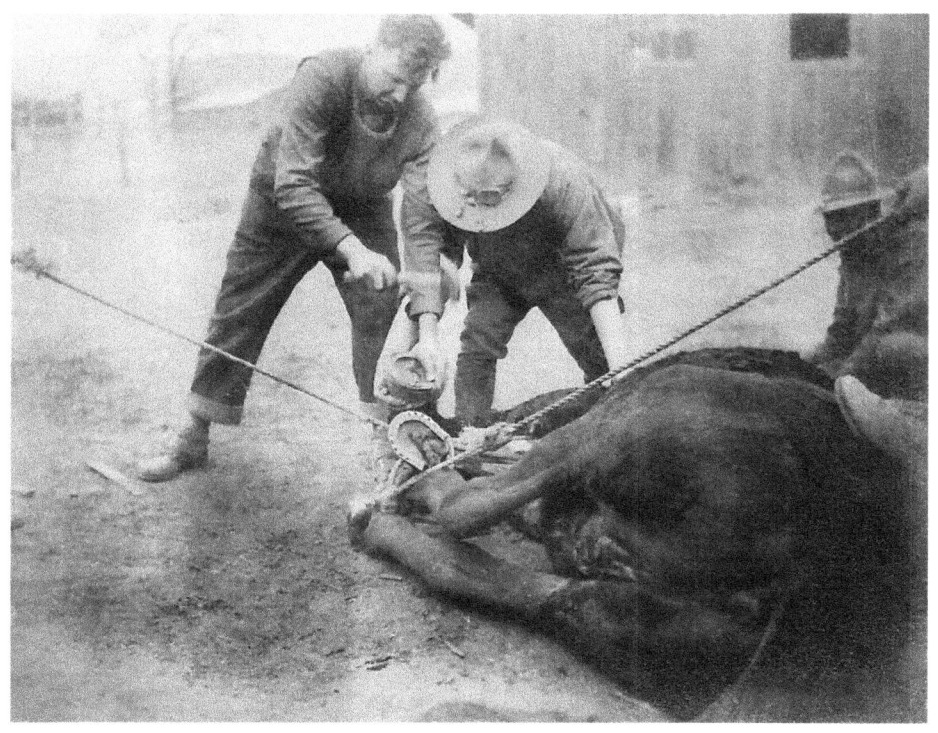

In this picture, Herb Short and an unidentified soldier are shoeing a horse by wrapping a rope around its rump, pulling it to the ground, and hobbling it, a method that was necessary for a green-broke horse.
(Courtesy of the HS Collection)

Two pictures of some of the farriers during WWI (Courtesy of the HS Collection)

Animals of War

The use of animals in the Great War included more than horses. Young, strong homing pigeons, transported to the front in baskets by dogs, carried messages back to headquarters from both land and sea. Often the message was sent by two birds, thus increasing the odds of getting through. In fact, one man per tank was skilled in the training and use of these carrier pigeons. Perhaps the most heroic of these was Cher Ami, who though wounded, carried the message from the Lost Battalion back to division headquarters.

On October 3, 1918, the war was winding down. A force that later became known as the Lost Battalion became surrounded by Germans during the Battle of the Argonne Forest. Major Charles White Whittlesey and several hundred men had no food or ammunition and were being fired upon by their own artillery. Major Whittlesey attempted to send four homing pigeons, each carrying a message, to their artillery. The first two pigeons were shot down, and the third one's message contained the wrong coordinates. The last pigeon, Cher Ami, was shot but after twenty-five minutes, he succeeded in delivering his message and saved the lives of all the trapped men.

Cher Ami was blinded in one eye and was hit in the leg. Army medics saved him and made a wooden leg for him. He was sent to the United States and was named mascot of the Department of Service and was awarded the Croix de Guerre medal and the gold medal from the Organized Bodies of American Racing Pigeon Fanciers. After his death, Cher Ami's body was mounted and placed in the Smithsonian Institution.

Cher Ami as photographed on April 22, 1919,
shortly after arriving in the United States
(Courtesy of National Archives)

Another heroic animal of WWI was a dog named Stubby. While he was on guard duty, he caught a German spy, biting him until the Allied troops captured him. As a result, Stubby was the first dog to be promoted to sergeant. In April 1918 Stubby's unit was attacked by the Germans near Seicheprey, France. Stubby was wounded and became a therapy dog at the Red Cross hospital. He later was involved in the liberation of a French town, whose women made him a blanket and medals. Stubby died in March 1926 and was preserved by taxidermy. He was given to the Smithsonian and is part of "The Price of Freedom" exhibit.

Sergeant Stubby: The Most Decorated War Dog of World War I
(Public domain picture)

Although animals were often used to deliver both messages and rations to the front, soldiers on bicycles also performed this dangerous mission.

George Samuels of Cedar Gap and an unidentified soldier would deliver messages from the telephone lines to the soldiers fighting at the front.

(Courtesy of the MAHS Collection)

August 26, 1918

John A. Hensley and wife

Dear Parents,

Your letter received today and was glad to know everybody is all right. I am feeling fine and am having it pretty easy so far, have been in the army over a month, and so far I haven't earned a dime. I have been assigned to the mounted orderly section but have never been assigned a horse and saddle yet. Each orderly has charge of two horses, one for himself, and one for some officer. All they have to do is take care of the two horses, ride around with the officers, and carry their messages. We don't have to do guard duty, or kitchen police, or drill and hike, so you see we get out of the real hard duties of army life.

So far, I have just been helping take care of the horses, about two hours' work in the morning, then we are off til 2:00 to 3:00 in the afternoon; then we go to school at the Kansas building. We are learning signal work and learning how to carry messages, as that will be our main duty, if we see any overseas duty. We will be mounted as long as we stay here but will not use any horses when we get over. The rumor here is that we are going to Russia, of course, we can't tell anything by what we hear, as the Camp (Camp Funston, Kansas) is full of rumors. We have been hearing for some time that we are to be transferred to Camp Kearney, Calif., then to Russia. You never know what to believe, but I wouldn't be surprised if we don't leave here before long. I don't think anybody would care, as none of us like this dusty, hot country; it's the sand storms we don't like, makes it so hard to keep clean. Am with a bunch of fine fellows. They are all special service men, such as electricians, mechanics, clerks, and musicians as the band is quartered here and the Headquarters Co. is always the best company in a regiment.

The sergeant just told me he was going to give me a horse and send me out on drill field with a French officer – am anxious to go out and watch them drill. Haven't been on a hike since I was transferred from the depot brigade. I have a rifle, canteen but have never used them any yet. All men are issued rifles, etc.

Tell Otto to come up any Saturday or Sunday and I can get off til Monday morning. Saturday and Sunday are visitors' days – and thousands of people are here then; we can go any place we want to by getting a 36-hour pass. I think I shall try for a furlough about October 1, if we are here then. It's pretty hard to get a furlough and they always investigate before issuing them, but from what they say, it's easier to get a farm furlough than any other kind. Tell Otto if he comes to call for me at building 1137.

The 10th Division had a big review here Saturday; sure was some sight. There were nearly 40,000 in it, and you could see soldiers as far as you could look in any direction. We have plenty to eat - yesterday we had chicken and ice cream for dinner; sometimes we are a little shy, but it's because they can't get it in time – most of the time we are well fed. We go to bed at 10:30 and get up at 5:30. I am getting used to it and feel good all the time if it wasn't so hot.

We signed payroll this morning so we will have a pay day soon. I will have $22.10 due me. My insurance costs me $6.60 and my laundry $1 per month; we are allowed to send 15 pieces each week, so we don't have to do any washing, as they take it out of your pay whether you send any or not.

Answer soon,

R. C. Hensley

Headqrs Co.

41 Inf.

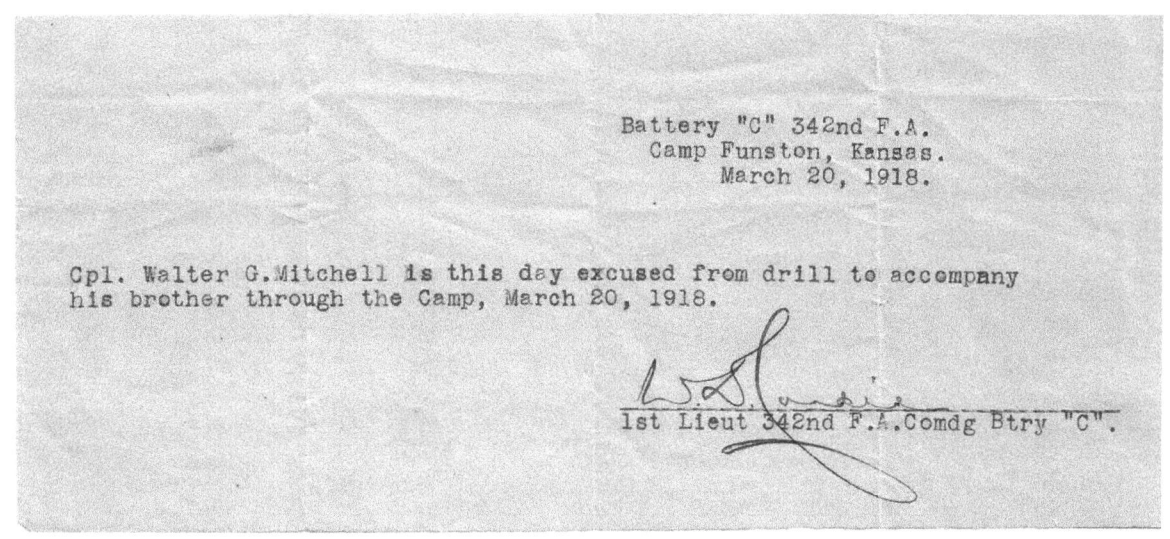

Sample of a pass for leave. (Courtesy of the KDG Collection)

Payroll line at Camp Funston at Ft. Riley, Kansas (Courtesy of the MAHS Collection)

Leisure Time

August 30, 1918
Paris Island, S.C.

Editor Mansfield Mirror,

I suppose it is quite a surprise to the people of Mansfield at my joining the Marines but I held off just as long as I could. I am located on an island about two miles off the mainland from Port Royal. There are four ports to the island. First is the quarantine camp where we waited for examination and received our outfit. From there we marched seven miles south where we are now. This is one of the barracks. From here we go to the main barracks and from there to the rifle range. This place is a pretty nice place to be. We get nearly all of our drill and bayonet practice here. We also have a drill called Swedish. This is more sport than anything. We go out and have games of all sorts; also boxing, wrestling, racing, rope climbing, and bar work, such as chinning bars, and bars for testing arms and shoulders. The Swedish tests every muscle in the body. We have an arm and leg drill every morning before breakfast, which gives us a good appetite. We also play baseball, basketball, and football.

We have a lot of work to do but it is a kind of work that is interesting, because you are always learning something new. A man is a man when he gets through here. Gambling is something you never see here in the Marines. We have a real good Y.M.C.A. and churches of all kinds.

We also have a naval hospital here. I have had a little experience with it. I had a small operation performed on my leg for an abscess which kept me out of drill for 3 days, but I am well now. I would be glad to hear from you people at any time as letters here are few.

I like the life fine and expect to stay with it quite a while yet. I enlisted as a drummer and I expect to be placed with a Marine band in a few weeks. The Marines here have a swell band. They do parade work and play for "colors" twice a day. Our company was out on parade the other night but I was not able to be with them. The corporal sent me out as company inspector to see if they marched in a straight line as they passed the mayor.

I must close. I would be pleased to get a copy of the Mirror if you have one left over.

Yours truly,

Private Jos. D. Mashburn

322 Co., Bat. R., U.S.M.C.

Paris Island, S. C.

Boxing served as a means of physical training for our troops. It was used to build physical strength, increase morale, provide entertainment, and prepare the soldiers for warfare. The YMCA organized and promoted boxing matches both stateside and in military camps.

Herb Short boxing with a fellow soldier (Courtesy of the HS Collection)

Soldiers would frequently spend their spare time playing craps and other games. Clyde Tarbutton is the soldier in the center. (Courtesy of the HS Collection)

"We see soldiers here from all the Allied nations, but the khaki clad boys from the dear old USA outnumber them all."

Orie Walton, Somewhere in France. (*Mansfield Mirror* Oct. 10, 1918)

September 1918

Over There and Back Home

Back Home:

"Snippets from Home"

"The Red Cross met Tuesday afternoon in their workroom. The helpless case shirts were finished. The new work at hand is the trench foot slipper." (*Mansfield Mirror* Sept 5, 1918)

Overseas Red Cross volunteers often penned letters for our wounded soldiers. These might have been their last words to loved ones back home.

(Public domain picture)

"Mansfield Public Schools opened with 209 students." (*Mansfield Mirror* Sept 5, 1918)

"Otis Dedmon, the son of William Dedmon and wife, in the Pea Ridge neighborhood, died Thursday from diphtheria." (*Mansfield Mirror* Sept 5, 1918)

"A telegram was received yesterday afternoon by W.A. Black, secretary of Mansfield's Seventh Annual Agricultural & Stock Show, from Congressman Thos. L. Rubey at Washington stating that he had secured a government airplane for the fair. This will prove a decided attraction and draw an unusually large attendance for the World's Fair of the Ozarks. The securing of the airplane for exhibition flights, together with the patriotic day program, will certainly be appreciated." (*Mansfield Mirror* Sept. 5, 1918)

"Miss Sarah Gaskill, county chairman of War records, has the county well organized. At last report 1344 men enlisted in the service from Wright County." (*Mansfield Mirror* Sept 12, 1918)

"Mrs. G. Akers received a letter from her two boys-one from France and one from Germany. They are ok but the one in Germany is a little hungry." (*Mansfield Mirror* Sept. 12, 1918)

We had gone to war in Europe more than a year ago and although most minor leagues closed, only a handful of major league players had been drafted or had enlisted. But that all changed in July when the Provost Marshall General, Enoch Crowder, a Missouri native, decreed that men in "non-essential" occupations must be draft-eligible or enlist to help stateside. Consequently, the schedule was reduced from 154 to 140 games. However, special consideration was given to the two World Series teams, the Chicago Cubs and the Boston Red Sox. Mansfield's native son, Carl Mays, was pitching for the Red Sox.

"Mr. and Mrs. G. C. Freeman returned from a trip to Chicago to visit relatives and saw the Boston Red Sox defeat Chicago 2 to 1 in the World Series. Carl Mays of Mansfield pitched Saturday for the Red Sox and won the game 2 to1. G. C. Freeman is the proud possessor of the ball Mays used when he put the last man out-winning the game- presented to him by the famous pitcher." (*Mansfield Mirror* Sept 12, 1918)

Carl Mays when he was playing for the Boston Red Sox

(Courtesy of Larry Dennis)

Incidentally, the *Star-Spangled Banner* was played at a big-league game for one of the first times, starting a tradition that we continue today.

"Mansfield England is prepared to show Mansfield boys, who are in Europe, all the possible comforts, it is learned from a letter received by Mayor W. G. Reynolds from Mansfield in England. Boys from every Mansfield in the United States are to be made especially welcome. Similar letters being sent to the mayor of every town named Mansfield in the United States." (*Mansfield Mirror* Sept 19, 1918)

"In the county 1836 men are registered, of whom 1828 were native born; 5, naturalized; 2 citizens by father's naturalization before registrant's majority and 1 non declarant alien." (*Mansfield Mirror* Sept 19, 1918)

"Lots of tomatoes are being processed by the various canning factories. J. W. Kennedy & Sons are now operating 4 factories, at Hartville, Norwood, Macomb, and Talmage. The Roberts & Elder Kanning Ko. was located at Bryant." (*Mansfield Mirror* Sept 19, 1918)

"The first car of ore to be shipped from the Mansfield mining district since the two mills – the Red Bird and the Pioneer - have been in operation here, was a car of jack billed out today to Joplin by the Pioneer Mining Co. A. J. Clark, president of company, went to Joplin this morning on business connected with the shipment." (*Mansfield Mirror* Sept 19, 1918)

"Two months ago, Carl Mays, pitcher with the Boston Red Sox, had a fine chance to secure a commission in the Aviation Corps but passed this up in order to help the Sox win the pennant and subsequent championship. Carl is making plans at once to auction off all the cattle of his ranch and then enter the Army." (*Mansfield Mirror* Sept 26, 1918)

Carl was subsequently drafted from Douglas County, Missouri. Years later, Carl told family members of his draft experience. "I got notice in the mail that I was to pick up 21 boys and take them and go to St. Louis and go into the Army. That was the year that the flu was so bad. On Wednesday we left and on Monday morning there were 11 of them dead." Carl contracted and survived the flu. The signing of the Armistice enabled him to rejoin his wife and prepare for the following baseball season.

Over There:

September 9, 1918

Dear Folks at Home:

Your letter dated August 8th received today. Sure was glad to hear from home again. How's everything with you? Have been moving around again since I last wrote you. This is Sunday afternoon and I haven't anything to do at present so I will write you a few words.

Sorry to hear of the dry weather at home, was in hopes the season would continue to be good, as long as it started out to be. Everything here is looking good as far as I can see. Would like to hear from Silas. Gee, guess he thinks he is making big money. Well, it is good money, glad he is liking it fine for I was afraid that he would work too hard and him not used to anything like he is in now.

Have been moving around so fast that my mail has a time keeping up. Tell Silas I would like to swap jobs with him. Can't say why I don't get more of your letters, I get about ½ the mail that is sent out from there as I get a letter from some folks and they tell me about writing letters that I never got, and some of yours I get a way late. That's the way my mail comes, sorter in a bunch. Try to write so you will hear at least once a week. Seems as I can get the letters that you write last first. Yes, wish I could tell you every day how I was but can't do that. Living in hope that everything is well with you. Am glad that Mama is better; not that I had heard anything about her being sick, but guess I am just as well as if I had known it. Hope she and all the rest will hold your good health. Couldn't ask for better health for myself. Glad you saved my policy. Will send you some money when we get paid again as guess you have used about all I had in the bank. Haven't made another allotment yet; think I will before long.

Yes, Homer is still with me; see him every day almost. Told him what you said and he said he would write them a letter. Tell them he is well and looking fine. All the boys from around home are looking good. Saw Frank Hoover and Walter Coday the other day. All was feeling good. Glad you get the good news from homeboys, guess you know as much as I do for I hardly ever see a paper anymore. Staying with the Lord and will as long as I live for I think He is a great helper in time of need. Never forget to ask His blessings on those at home. I know that you at home think and worry more about me than I do myself. By all asking and believing we will come through all right. Do you ever get any of mail that is cut out? Tell all hello.

With love to all,
Clifford M. Seal
Hdqrs Co. 129 F.A.
American E. Forces

September 19, 1918

Camp Funston, Kansas

Dear Sister,

I will write you a few lines to let you know that I am fine and dandy. Hope you all are the same. It has been raining here for two days. It has turned cooler now. I haven't had much to do today, except stand inspection. I passed alright. I am on fatigue duty tomorrow. I don't like to work on Sunday, but I am in the army now and not behind the plow.

I signed up for three liberty bonds this morning $150 worth, on the allotment plan; that will be $15 per month, for nine months, ending in July next. The bonds are made to you and when they are paid in full, which will be next July, they bear 4 1/4%. I think I was the only man in our company who took that much except the officers. Our company took $6,550 worth of bonds. I will draw only $7.40 per month now.

I sure have a lot of clothing. I have two pairs of shoes, six pairs of socks, three suits of underwear, two pairs of pants, two shirts, one jacket, one overcoat, one slicker, one suit of unionalls, two pairs of leggings, three towels, one shaving outfit. Three blankets, one cot and mattress, one haversack, one pack carrier, canteen and cover, one belt holding 240 rounds of ammunition, one rifle and bayonet, one barrack bag; so you see I have some outfit. I don't know when we will leave here, but we are expecting to leave most any time.

Well, tell everybody hello for me. It is about time for taps. I will have to go to bed, so goodbye.

Your brother,

Private Roy L. Hensley,

Co. F, 70th Inf.

```
✣ ✣ ✣ ✣ ✣ ✣ ✣ ✣ ✣ ✣ ✣ ✣ ✣
✣  Equipment of the United States  ✣
✣  Infantryman costs $156.71.       ✣
✣  One bedsack ............$   .89  ✣
✣  Three wool blankets ..... 18.75  ✣
✣  One waist belt ..........   .25  ✣
✣  Two pairs wool breeches.  8.90   ✣
✣  Two wool service coats ..15.20   ✣
✣  One hat cord ............   .08  ✣
✣  Three pairs summer draw-          ✣
✣    ers ....................  1.50 ✣
✣  Three pairs winter draw-          ✣
✣    ers ....................  3.88 ✣
✣  One pair wool gloves ....   .61  ✣
✣  One service hat .......... 1.70  ✣
✣  Two pairs extra shoe laces   .05 ✣
✣  Two pairs canvas leggins.  1.05  ✣
✣  Two flannel shirts .......  7.28 ✣
✣  Two pairs shoes .......... 10.20 ✣
✣  Five pairs wool stockings. 1.50  ✣
✣  Four identification tags..   .02 ✣
✣  Summer undershirts .....   1.50  ✣
✣  Four winter undershirts..  4.88  ✣
✣  One overcoat ............ 14.92  ✣
✣  Five shelter tent pins ...   .29 ✣
✣  One shelter tent pole ....   .26 ✣
✣  One poncho .............   3.58  ✣
✣  One shelter tent ........  2.95  ✣
✣  One rifle ............... 19.50  ✣
✣  One bayonet ............   2.15  ✣
✣  One bayonet scabbard ...   1.13  ✣
✣  One cartridge belt ......  4.08  ✣
✣  100 cartridges ..........  5.00  ✣
✣  One steel helmet .......   3.00  ✣
✣  One gas mask ........... 12.00   ✣
✣  One trench tool .........   .50  ✣
✣                          ───────  ✣
✣     Total ............... $156.71 ✣
```

A photo of Roy Hensley
(Courtesy of Teresa Cantrell)

(*Mansfield Mirror* Feb. 14, 1918)

September 29, 1918

Somewhere in France

Dear Ones at Home,

I received your letter dated August 28 and sure was glad to hear you were all well at home. I am well and feeling fine, getting along fine, like army life better every day, although shells fall all around us, but we don't mind that.

I was eating breakfast one morning when a 155 lit about 50 feet from us and filled my coffee cup full of mud, so that is all the damage the Dutch has done me out of lots of shells. We can hear the German shells a long ways off. But those Austria whiz-bangs slip up on us. We got three men killed the first day, but we have made the Dutch pay for that several times, and they are on the run and can't stop until they get to Berlin.

You asked if any of the boys were here that I knew. Yes, Newt Sanders, Arthur Roper, Jim Tefteller, Illie Williams, John Canifax and several Douglas County boys. We have lots of fun in spite of all the shells for we see lots of air fights. I have helped bury one Dutchman. Oh, yes, I am cooking at battalion headquarters, and I gathered a big pot of green beans out of a Dutch garden and had them for dinner two or three days ago. Tell Grandpa I can't tell how they used to do, only they're hunting hogs in this country for us to get so we can have fresh meat, but lots of bacon.

Well, I haven't got any bugs, lots of the boys have - there are lots here. Well, I can hear the big boys asking the Dutch to move back, and believe me, they are going too and they don't have any idea where they can stop, and this is a bad night; it is raining and cold. Well, I have sure got three good friends: my 45, my gas mask, and steel hat. My hat protects my head; my mask- my lungs, and my 45 gets the Hun.

Well, tell Pa that I know he got lots to eat while he was threshing, but he hasn't got me skinned a bit. We sure do have lots to eat. Well, you should have seen me the first day of my real experience. I was riding one horse and leading one down a road and a Dutchman in an aeroplane turned a machine gun on me and the way I went wasn't slow. I think about it now and laugh. But he missed me by a little. Oh, yes, and Herbert Short is here, too. He is just a little ways from here and is getting along fine as far as I know. Have Jason and Robert been called yet? I don't think any of the last draft will have to come over here; if they do, they won't have much to do, I think. I think that the big time is about over, anyway. Where did Ernie Crippen go for training and what is his address? Well, I know you sure had a nice visit with Aunt Lindia and Elvira. I am glad they made you a visit.

Well, it is Sunday and I will finish your letter as shells were plentiful last night. Fritz is still hammering away, but he shoots a while then runs a while and I think his shooting is almost done as he doesn't scare the Sammies a bit by bursting big shells around them. We sure have a big time in spite of all Fritz can do, but I must say this is a torn up place. This battlefield sure looks bad. You can find anything you want to look for, from a pistol to a cannon. The ground is decorated with German helmets and Dutch guns.

Well, I would like to see you all but this soldiering has to be done and I like it fine. I know it is dangerous but it is lots of fun to see the Dutchman get out of his trench and run for his life and throw up his hands and yell, "Comrade". Well I think we will be in Germany in a very short time and you know that will mean, "Get out, Dutchmen!"

Say, can you tell Harley's and Uncle Wesley's folks and Uncle Gordon's that they will have to excuse me for not writing as they can hear through you folks, but for them to write just the same. Has Hosie come back home to live? Tell me all the news. Well, I will close and try to write more next time. So goodbye and good luck.

Your son,
Ira C. Stout
Headquarters Co. 341 F.A., America

Soldiers on the Western Front battled on the front line for approximately a week and then moved further back to assist with the supply line. Getting the necessary supplies to the front was a never-ending process.

Lice infestations were commonplace in the trenches as were rats, disease, and mud. In some cases, heavy rains turned the trenches into quagmires. The Sanitation Corps soldiers were trained in disease prevention and maintaining good hygiene, both in training camps and on the front lines.

The Sanitary Train operated in three separate areas. Located approximately 500 to 1500 yards behind the front lines were three Battalion Aid Stations. Another 300 yards back were the Ambulance Section Dressing Stations. Finally, the four field hospitals were located 2 to 4 miles behind the front lines. These separate units acted systematically and progressively to treat and evacuate the wounded.

Along the southern portion of the Western Front, the Germans withdrew, and in less than two days the Americans took 15,000 prisoners and captured over 400 pieces of artillery. However, in the corridor between the Meuse River and the Argonne Forest the Germans did not fall back. The Meuse-Argonne Offensive, also known as the Battle of the Argonne Forest, resulted in the most U.S. military deaths in the field. An estimated 26,000 American casualties resulted.

October 1918

Over There and Back Home

October 3, 1918

Somewhere in France

We were about 7 ½ days on the waters. We were near Amiens when they were bombing it. Things are higher here than milk was when the cow jumped over the moon. Haven't seen a stalk of corn since leaving Arkansas. Freezing this morning, about 3,500 feet above sea level the wind blows pretty cold. It rains nearly every day. We are digging trenches. The last Mirror I saw was the May 30th issue.

Marvin H. Dennis

110th Engineers

Soldiers, probably farriers due to the knives they are carrying, pose above some trenches. The farriers would have to use their long knives in the euthanizing of wounded horses. (Courtesy of the HS Collection)

October 8, 1918
Somewhere in France

Dear Home Folks,

Hello to all. How are all at home? I'm OK. I have received several letters from you since I wrote you last, some of them on the battlefield.

We made a big drive, I guess you will read all about it before you get this letter. The battlefield is something awful to see – the dead and wounded. I have had to drive my team out of the road and pick my way through the dead soldiers to keep from driving over them. I have had several close calls myself. I was under a tree trying to shelter myself from the flying shrapnel when one cut the top out and hit one team that was also under the tree, but myself and team got out ok.

I have seen several prisoners. I got enough gas to make my mouth sore, or I think that is what is the matter for I run into gas once before I could get my mask on. All the boys that I know from back home made it through as far as I know.

I guess Annie and Eulalla are getting rich now. I have two letters from Annie since she went to Springfield. Clyde said for you to tell his folks that it was not his fault that they did not hear from him, as he had been writing to them. I guess father is about through his assessing by this time, is he not? How's Reba making it at school now?

I am in a town, but I don't know the name of it, and if I did, I could not write it, for the letter would be destroyed. Well, I can't think of any more to write, only you can tell the people back there that has boys over here, that they have taken desperate chances for their lives in the last drive, you will get that news in the papers. I have seen the ground blown up so badly that you could not get through with a wagon and team for the shell holes, but still more shells falling, and nowhere but a shell hole to go to for safety. I will close and write again soon.

Wag. Claude E. Tripp
Supply Co., 140th Infantry

Dear Friends of Missouri,

I will take the pleasure of writing you a few lines and describe the branch of service that I am in. The tank service sure is a fine branch of service, six large guns on the inside of one tank – three of them are machine guns. They get so hot on the inside a fellow can't stay in them very long at a time.

We usually take two hikes each week – some hikes too – but they are good for a fellow. The weather here is fine, nice and warm. Crops look fine, cotton fields as far as your eyes will let you see.

As ever I remain,
Geo. Shores
Co. B., 305 Bat.
Raleigh, N. C.
(*Mansfield Mirror* Oct 24, 1918)

Back Home:

Spanish Flu

"Due to the epidemic of Spanish Flu the management of the Nugget Theatre has voluntarily closed. The schools are closed. In some homes every member of the family is suffering." (*Mansfield Mirror* Oct 10, 1918)

The first Spanish Flu obituaries appeared in the October 10, 1918, edition of the *Mansfield Mirror* and listed Inez Westbrook, 39 years, Mrs. M.E. Dennis, 24 years, Miss Gertrude Fuson, daughter of Dr. F. B. Fuson, living in Washington D. C., and Henry Bogart, 41 of Springfield, formerly of Douglas County.

Only one week later, twenty-two death notices/obituaries related to the Spanish Flu epidemic were published, and seven were men in service stateside in army training camps.

The October 24 issue of the *Mirror* carried the erroneous news that Mr. and Mrs. Sherman Helsley died of influenza. The following edition carried the corrected information that it was not the parents, but their baby who had died.

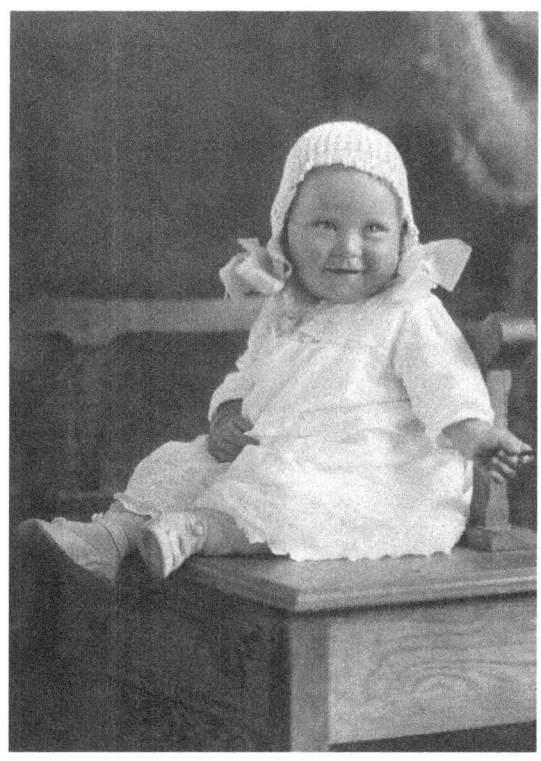

Hershel Helsley, son of Mr. & Mrs. Sherman Helsley, died from influenza in Oct. 1918.

(Courtesy of the AD Collection)

"Mrs. A. J. Wilder has returned from her trip to Kansas City and St. Louis. She was accompanied on her trip by her daughter, Mrs. Rose Wilder Lane, who has been called to London to do publicity work for the Red Cross." (*Mansfield Mirror* Oct 17, 1918)

The railroad played a crucial role in Mansfield as it transported our troops to war and carried back home the casualties, both war-related and those who succumbed to illness. "James Alfred Duckworth, a Douglas County boy, who died of pneumonia at Ft. Brady, Mich. was shipped back home for burial, the body arriving here in Mansfield by rail last Tuesday." (*Mansfield Mirror* Oct. 24, 1918)

"William Grover Reynolds, mayor of Mansfield, the only son of J. D. Reynolds of Ava, 30 years old, died in Kansas City, having gone there on business. The remains were shipped here on Monday and the body was taken to his home – Oakwood Place. Interment taking place on Tuesday in the Reynolds' family burying ground, adjoining the Mansfield cemetery. He was a member of the Modern Woodsman of America. His funeral was conducted at the residence of Rev. John T. Younger of the Cumberland Presbyterian Church." (*Mansfield Mirror* Oct. 24, 1918)

Reynolds tombstone   Oakwood Place

"Snippets from Home"

News from Berlin Coday: We completed our two-month training in the Rahe Auto School, but so far have not driven any. They have several horses and mules here and it looks like we might just drive them instead." (*Mansfield Mirror* Oct 24, 1918)

"Yes, we had a little snow this morning and if you had been looking you might have seen housewives gathering green beans in the snow." (*Mansfield Mirror* Oct 24, 1918)

"The body of Curtis K. Denney of the 210th Engineers, a Douglas County boy who died Friday of bronchial pneumonia at Camp Funston, Kas., arrived here Monday en-route to his home for interment, accompanied by F. E. Chandler, of the same company." (*Mansfield Mirror* Oct 24,1918)

"The *Mountain Grove Journal* reports the death of Bernie Eberhardt of the navy and of Everett Leach of the marines in Maryland and of Maynard Thorne at Camp MacArthur, Texas, and of Yaslav Liska at Camp Dodge, Ia." (*Mansfield Mirror* Oct 24, 1918)

"Jeff Newton was at Camp Funston during the week to see his son, Mose, who is sick with pneumonia." (*Mansfield Mirror* Oct 31, 1918)

October 19, 1918

Stateside

My Dear Homefolks,

I have received several letters and also the package which was very much appreciated. The cookies were fine, the best I ever ate. I can truthfully say. I sure like my sweater, I guess you are all well. I am feeling as good as ever but still have some cold, had the earache the other day. I guess you got my picture by this time. I sent one to Lola and Hazel. Probably send the others home with my suitcase.

The influenza seems to be coming to a close here. I hope so. The boys in the northern camps have suffered more than we have. It seems to be at a turning point. I hate to hear of so many deaths around home. You must take good care of yourselves. I wish I could be home to help with the work, I know my help is needed so bad. I think I will be home soon the way things are looking now, but we can't tell yet. We may be sent over, if peace is made, for guards.

I went out to a fire last night and saw the fire police work, I ran out there a mile. It destroyed a barn and some straw, not much damage done.

We get our O.D. Clothes (olive drab) tomorrow. Do not write anymore as we go east to Camp Dick, N.J. the first of the week. I will write along the different places to let you know how I am. I am transferred as a bugler. You know I didn't know for some time, but I know now. Hoping you are all well.

I remain your loving son and brother,

Carl M. Henson

Camp McArthur

Waco, Texas

October 29, 1918

Dear Homefolks,

I will drop you a few lines as I can now take time. I am on special duty, am watching the registered mail in this orderly room, so I get to use the typewriter. Well, I guess some of you wonder why I never write. I tell you since I came to the army I get so much mail I have had all my spare time taken up writing, but you believe me it makes one feel so good to get letters from home. I wish sometimes everybody would write to me. Well, you want to know something about army life. I know well it is a great life if you don't weaken. I have been in the hospital for 23 days. I had the influenza and oh, boy, it sure got my goat. There has been over a thousand of the boys here died. I was one of the lucky boys to get out. Oh, I sure would love to be home for a few days, I sure could enjoy myself, but it won't be long now, I think, for Kaiser Bill has got his fill. Oh, If I could get him on my bayonet, I would end the war before long. Well, we are not having as tough a time as the depot brigade boys. I am in the 10th Division and will be with the boys over in France before long; but the boys in the depot brigade won't get to go over seas. I may not, but think I will. We have a

Y.M.C.A. with us wherever we go to write and pass the time when we are off duty. Everything at the Y.M.C.A is as free as the water. They have shows and speakings.

The Army is not too bad after the first ten years. I have been in the service for over three months and I have had some real good times along with the bad. Of course, we would all like to be at home with our wives. I would, but I know I feel better than some of the fellows.

Well, I guess I have said about enough. I could keep this foolishness up the rest of the night, though it is now 4:30 in the morning. I have to finish training for the gas tomorrow; I go through the gas house. One looks awful with a gas mask on. We look like a bunch of frogs but the experience is worth our lives in No Man's Land.

Well, it has been raining here awful bad, but it is clear this morning. I want you all to pray for me when I get to the front; I must close for this time, as I am looking to be relieved. I am in charge of quarters today so I won't get to sleep until I make the boys clean the barracks up.

Well, good night,
Private James H. Cameron
Company C,
210th Engineers
Camp Funston, Kansas

World War I soldier wearing gas mask
(Courtesy of pixels.com)

"We call our gun Father and our gas mask Mother."

Ira Stout A.E.F. in France (*Mansfield Mirror* Dec.19, 1918)

November 1918

Over There and Back Home

Back Home:

"False reports of the war being over: Mansfield celebrates with bonfires and parades, the blowing of whistles, the ringing of bells and discharging of firearms. Mansfield, in common with New York, St. Louis, Springfield, and other cities, today celebrated the report that the war was over, but no official verification of the report has been received at press time. The school children and others marched around the square. J. W. Gilley was also on hand with his big flag." (*Mansfield Mirror* Nov 7, 1918)

For America the Great War, as it was known then, lasted 4 years, 4 months, and 14 days when peace was declared with the signing of the Armistice in France on November 11, 1918, thereby declaring a cease fire until the terms of permanent peace were decided.

"At an early hour Monday morning our citizens were awakened by the ringing of the bells and the blowing of whistles, and a big noise in general, celebrating the close of the war, the surrender of Germany being confirmed. Flags and decorated cars added to the occasion and the firing of guns made plenty of noise. Hostilities ceased at the eleventh hour of the eleventh day of the eleventh month." (*Mansfield Mirror* Nov 14, 1918)

"Frank Mays arrived home Saturday on furlough from New York where he has been recovering from injuries received while en-route to France. The boat on which he was sailing was torpedoed and his right ear and his left eye suffered injuries, affecting his sight and hearing. He was rescued and taken to a French hospital where he spent some time before returning to the U.S." (*Mansfield Mirror* November 21, 1918)

November 17, 1918

France

Dear Mother and All,

I have been moving around some and haven't had time to write, but I'm still OK, and Mother Dear, it is all over. About all we talk about now is when do we start home. I haven't had any mail for over a month. I wrote to Raymond and Virgil some time ago, but haven't had an answer and don't know where they are, but hope they are all right.

It is pretty cold here and there is a heavy frost every night. I've almost forgotten what a fire looks like, but we have plenty to eat so we get along fine. I was on my way to the front when the fighting stopped, so I didn't get in on the real stuff. I finished school and have a card that says "excellent operation" so I was ready to do my part.

I am in St. Romain, a small town close to St. Algnan, about the central part of France. We will be sent to some other outfit before long. I think to stay with and go back with to the states. We have a YMCA here and can buy hot chocolate at night which tastes fine and sometimes they have cookies too. Mother, you can't imagine what a paradise it will be to us when we get home.

Love to All,

Pvt Archie J. Miller

Hdqs Co., 164th Inf., APO 727

American E. Forces\41 Inf.

November 19, 1918

Belgium

Dear Home Folks,

I haven't had a letter from you for a couple of weeks, but will write again to tell you I am OK and getting along fine. Hope the Spanish Influenza isn't in your section of the country. I have heard so much about it from the States for the past month that it makes me anxious when I don't get a letter each week. I always write home once a week, but I haven't been able to the last two months on account of the scarcity of paper and moving about so much, but since the armistice, we have more time for writing and have been able to get paper.

I suppose there was a big time in the States about the 11th! You should have seen the people here in this country. The Yanks didn't put on much of a show, but the French and the Belgium citizens went wild. They acted like people released from a long prison term. As we moved forward they greeted us with smiling faces and "Viva American." They will do anything in the world for us and in some cases refuse money for things we buy. Refugees are coming through every day, going back to their homes. They have been held prisoners by Germans and made to work in munition factories. But some will only find a pile of stones and ashes where their beautiful homes existed. The men, women, and children pull and push carts with what little stuff they have on them. They work dogs, goats, and cows. Their horses and most of their cattle were taken by the Germans. One sight I will never forget was a man and woman pulling a harrow trying to cultivate a little ground so they might live.

The people almost cried as we marched into this town. They have the town all decorated with flags and with wreaths of flowers swinging clear across the street with signs of, "Welcome". We are billeted in what was a convent before the war but the Germans used the building for their horses. When we came in the Nuns were tickled to death. They wanted to scrub the windows but we wouldn't let them. They brought us a large table, benches, chairs, and coal and built us a fire and set up a stove where the boys had none. They heat water in the morning for us to wash with and come in all during the day to see if we have a fire and are comfortable. They can't do enough for us. Such kind, patient-hearted people, I never saw before. Such treatment makes a fellow feel like a man again after toughing it as we have for the last few months.

I don't know how long we will be here, but hear all kinds of rumors about going home, and say, an aeroplane will be too slow when we start home. But I expect to see some places of real interest before reaching the States. I expect to eat Easter dinner with you. Wishing you a Merry Christmas and a very Happy New Year.

Ever your son,

Pvt Raymond E. Miller

Co. F, 364th Inf. APO 776

American E. Forces

Back Home:

Peace Is Signed

As the news of victory circled the globe, Mansfield's citizens celebrated along with the rest of the world. The nation's leading publications touted the triumph of the Allies and the defeat of Germany as did the *Mansfield Mirror*.

"An 800-word message was received here today relative to the cancellation of the draft army. The boys who had been called to entrain Monday for the training camp returned home Tuesday morning because of the cablegram of peace declared. Those from Mansfield were Harley S. Williams, Noah Hylton, and Noah C. Smith." (*Mansfield Mirror* Nov 17, 1918)

Women wearing celebratory patriotic clothing
(Courtesy of the Bob Davis Collection)

Although, the Armistice was signed at 5:00 Paris time on November 11, 1918, when the State Department said that Germany gave in to the Allies' terms, men continued to give their lives in service to their country while news of lives lost in previous months are only now reaching home.

April 1919

Coming Home

The logistics of bringing our soldiers home took center stage following the signing of the Armistice. Peace had not been expected to occur for several months, and American troopships, as well as ships seized from Germany, were used to return troops to the United States from Europe. Most of our local boys were discharged and returned home by early summer 1919.

"New York, April 22 – They're coming home now. The heroes of the 35th Division and Missourians in New York, proud of the boys' achievements overseas, have prepared them a welcome. Heretofore casuals have drifted in now and then, but these days the boys are arriving in units, to hurriedly unload at Hoboken, whisked to Camp Merritt for a few days stay, and then sent to Camp Funston, Kans. for the demobilization. The 129th Field Artillery and the 110th Engineers are the first to arrive, both of them coming on ships that once flew the Kaiser's flag, the *Zeplin* and the *Von Steuben* respectively." (*Mansfield Mirror* April 24, 1919)

Company C., 110th Engineers, which included many of our area soldiers, returning from overseas on board the *U.S.S. von Steuben*, April 19, 1919, in Hoboken, N. J.

(National WWI Museum and Memorial, Kansas City, Missouri, USA.
https://theworldwar.org/explore/online-collections-database)

Our area men who served with the 110th Engineers: Sherman Borders, James "Tiny" Anderson Claxton, Ralph Dake, Marve Dennis, Ernest Elwood Gaskill, and William Richard Schlicher.

TRAVEL DATES OF COMPANY "A" 110TH ENGINEERS

April 1917	Organized
June 21	Mobilized at Washburn College
July 7	Topeka to Fort Riley, Kansas (The first National Guards called)
August 1	Fort Riley to Camp Funston
Oct. 18, 1918	Camp Funston, Kansas to Camp Doniphan, Oklahoma. (Fort Sill)
April 23	Left Fort Sill, Oklahoma for Port of Embarkation
April 27	Arrived Camp Merritt, New Jersey
April 30	Trip down the Hudson River, Boarded U.S.S. Great Northern
May 2	Towed out of harbor at 2:30 P.M. by Tugboat Newburg
May 10	Landed in France, Brest Harbor
May 14	Left Brest in freight cars (8 horses or 40 men)
May 15	Arrived Le Havre, Rest Camp No. 2 (English)
May 18	Left Le Havre, arrived at Eu. (Passenger Cars) Scottish Highlanders
May 19	Left Eu. Arrived St. Martin.
May 27	Left St. Martin. Arrived Coisy by Ailly sur Somme.
June 8	Left Coisy in French Freight Cars.
June 11	Arrived Derbigny, via Denoux.
July 1	Xertigny to Wesserling in Trucks.
July 4	Hiked up Boussat Hill.
July 7	The first Bombardment.
July 21	Arrived Camp McClure.
Sept. 1	Left Camp McClure. Arrived Chambray.
Sept. 5	Left Chambray. Arrived Blainville.
Sept. 6	Arrived Maron, after 42 Kilometer hike.
Sept. 10	Left Maron.
Sept. 11	Arrived Liverdun.
Sept. 12	In St. Mihiel Reserve.
Sept. 18	Left Liverdun. Arrived Charmont.
Sept. 20	Left Charmont.
Sept. 21	Arrived Beaulieu
Sept. 25	Advanced to Argonne Forest at No Man's Land in front of Sauquoit Hill.
Sept. 26	Barrage started at 2:30 A.M. Over the top at 5:00 A.M.
Oct. 1	Relieved by First Division.
Oct. 2	Left Chappy. To woods at Waly.
Oct. 5	Arrived at Conde. Where we received replacements.
Oct. 12	Left Conde.
Oct. 13	Arrived Monthairon.
Oct. 14	Arrived Camp Savoyards.
Nov. 6	Left Camp Savoyards.
Nov. 7	Arrived Ippecourt, by hike.
Nov. 9	Arrived Longchamps.
Nov. 10	Hiked to Loxeville-Ernecourt.
Nov. 11	Armistice signed.
Nov. 12	Hiked from Ernecourt to St. Mihiel.
Nov. 17	Hiked St. Mihiel to the woods north of Lacroix. (Fort De Tryon)
Dec. 9, 1919	Hiked to Lerouxville.

Feb. 8	Left Lerouxville for Brest via American Box Cars.
Feb. 12	Arrived Brest. 3:40 P.M. Hiked up hill to Pontenezen Barracks. (Tents)
Feb. 15	Deloused. Moved to Camp No. 4.
April 11	Left Brest, France via U.S.S. Von Steuben.
April 19	Arrived at New York, to Camp Mills.
April 27	Left Camp Mills.
April 30	Arrived Camp Funston after parading K.C., Mo., K.C., Kans. And Topeka, Kans.
May 3	Discharged to civilian life.

Thus ended the travels of Company "A" 110th Engineers. A.E.F.

(Public domain information)

POST-WAR HAPPENINGS

"Snippets from Home"

"Homecoming Reception to be held in the Mansfield City Park on July 4th, complete with a parade, entertainment, welcome address to be delivered by J. Lon Dennis, as well as response from the boys, our heroes." (*Mansfield Mirror* May 8, 1919)

"The Mansfield Concert Band and a large crowd of our people met the train yesterday morning on which W.C. Coday, Roy Handy, Claude Tripp, Clyde Tarbutton, Glenn Craig, and Frank Hoover arrived home. John Potts and Garrett Carter came in last night. These boys enlisted in what was formerly the Seymour Supply Co., later in the Supply Company of the 140th Infantry, and they saw a long service overseas." (*Mansfield Mirror* May 15, 1919)

American Legion

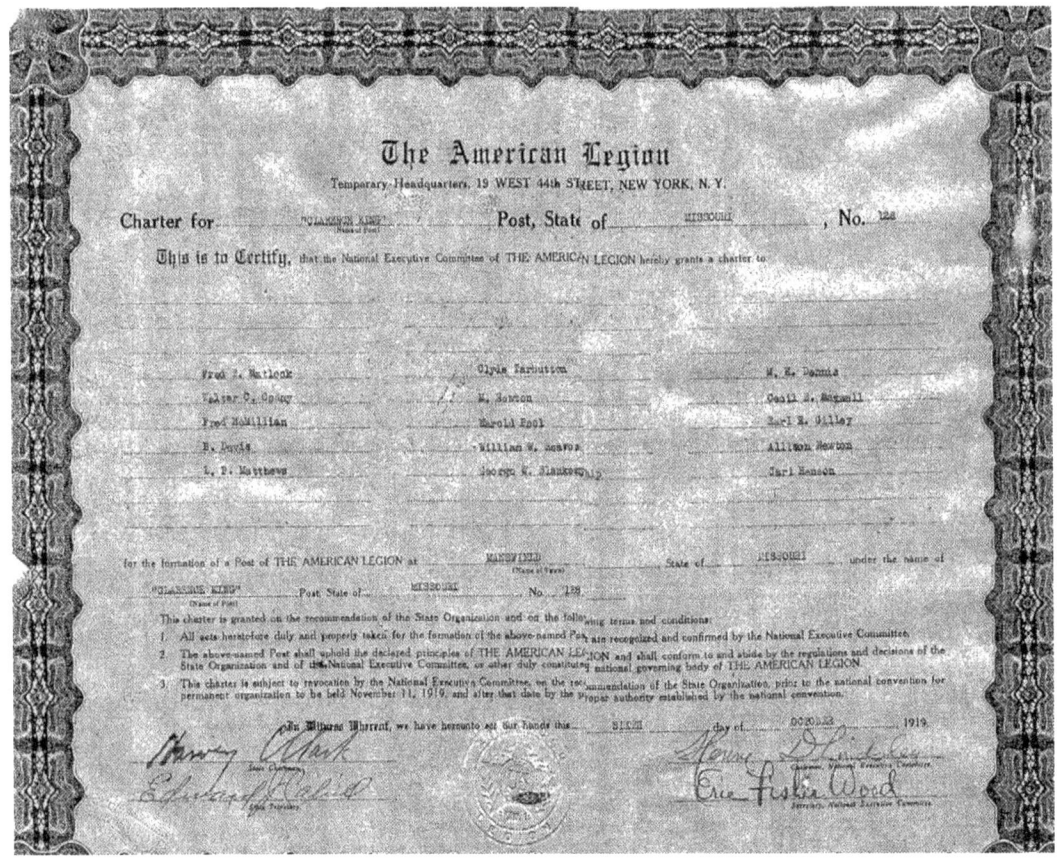

"In March 1919, The American Legion was founded in Paris, France, by members of the American Expeditionary Forces (A.E.F.) On September 16, 1919, the 66th U.S. Congress formally chartered The American Legion. In November 1919 the first convention of The American Legion was held in Minneapolis, Minnesota." *(American Legion – Wikipedia)*

"Paul Robinett returned from St. Louis Sunday after attending the first meeting of the Organized American Legion which was in session in St. Louis Thursday, Friday, and Saturday last week.

This organization is to be a fraternal, non-partisan organization with the sole object of promoting 100% Americanism. Those eligible are members of the Army, Navy, and Marine Corp. in the present war, G.A.R, veterans of the Indian Wars, and veterans of the Spanish American War.

E.C. Steele has been appointed Temporary Chairman and Paul Robinett, Vice-Chairman for Wright County. They have issued a call for a meeting of the eligibles of Wright County at the courthouse in Hartville, Saturday, May 24th, at 2:00 p.m. All persons eligible are urgently requested to be present and participate". (*Mansfield Mirror* May 15, 1919)

"At a meeting Saturday afternoon, Sept. 27, of ex-servicemen called together in honor of Col. Ruby D. Garrett and for the purpose of organizing a local post of the American Legion. We are very glad to state that the Colonel helped us to organize the post for the city of Mansfield which will be known as the Clarence King Post of the American Legion, the post being named in honor of Clarence King of Mansfield, who gave his all in the battle of the Argonne Forest, being a member of 140th Inf., 35th Division. The following names were enrolled as members: Fred T. Matlock, Walter C. Coday, Fred McMillian, Bob Davis, L.P. Matthews, Clyde Tarbutton, Mose Newton, Harold Pool, Wm. W. Reeves, Geo. W. Blankenship, Marvin H. Dennis, Earl Gilley, Cecil E. Maxwell, Allison Newton, Carl Henson, Andrew Goss, Charley R. Fry, George Bean, Jess C. Van Ness, Earnie N. Crippen, G. W. Moberly, Marvin R. Miller, Ovie E. Baker, Raymond Young, Oscar Freeman, Roy Handy. The following officers were elected: Walter C. Coday, Post Commander; Leroy P. Matthews, Vice Post Commander; Fred McMillian, Adjutant; Marvin H. Dennis, Finance Officer; Wm. W. Reeves, Historian; Harold Pool, Chaplain. All ex-servicemen are cordially invited to join the Clarence King Post, membership dues are $2 per year, payable to any of the first four officers. Snap it up and let's don't let the other towns beat Mansfield. Watch the Mirror for the meeting dates. – Fred McMillian, Adjutant." (*Mansfield Mirror* Oct 2, 1918).

More War News

Leon Tester, son of John Tester, was killed in the Battle in France, and several days ago his father was notified that the body of his son had arrived in New York and would be sent here. The body arrived at Mansfield September 16, 1921, and was taken to Hartville the next day. Then, it was taken to the home of his father near Little Creek. Services were held at Little Creek Church the following day. The casket was placed outside the church and the church was full and many more outside than inside. Burial was with Military Honors in Little Creek Cemetery. (www.ancestry.com)

"Homer Akers of Norwood is reported released from the German prison camp in which he has been confined." (*Mansfield Mirror* December 4, 1919)

In the following interview, Dr. Lieutenant Edens of Cabool shared his experience as a P.O.W. during World War I, detailing his injuries, captivity, and subsequent journey to safety, including his time in solitary confinement and the poor food rations.

Interview with Dr. Lieutenant Edens of Cabool, Former P.O.W.

"I was at a first aid post, fifty yards behind the front line dressing the wounds of a *Tommy." He further stated that they received a warning that the Huns were coming. Wounded were removed to a safer place and five minutes later the Huns came around the corner. "I was shot in the right arm." He went on to say that they threw in bombs, but he wasn't hit. They were then marched 20 miles to a hospital while under fire from both sides.

"I was put in solitary confinement in a hotel in Karlsruhe while being quizzed about the American army. I was then sent to the Russian officers' camp at Villingen. For the first three months the food was very bad. Thin soup most of the time made from field grass and a small piece of black bread every other day, and a piece of meat once a week was the ration. Sometimes it was seal meat and impossible to eat."

Germany did not release prisoners until November 30th til a special Red Cross train took them to France. On February 1st he reached New York and was discharged at Camp Dix. *(State Historical Society of Missouri/Digitized Newspaper Project/West Plains Journal February 20, 1919)*

* "Tommy" is a term for a British soldier.

Gold Star Mothers

American Gold Star Mothers is an organization composed of American mothers who have lost children who were serving in the Armed Forces. It began in 1928 and was named after the stars that were put on flags in family homes to represent their sons and daughters serving in the military. Living servicemen were honored with blue stars, while servicemen who had died were represented by gold stars.

The organization was formed by Grace Darling Seibold who lost her son during World War I. In the early 1930s, the US government formed groups of mothers and wives of lost soldiers and paid for their trips to France to pay homage to their loved ones.

HOME AT LAST

Clarence King's Obituary

"Mansfield's first soldier boy to make the supreme sacrifice in battle for the cause of liberty - for his own country and for the world, as well - is Clarence King, aged 18 years, son of Mrs. Mary Jane King Slate of Mansfield – and the name and life and actions of Clarence King will ever be fondly remembered by the people of Mansfield, The Holy Book says: "Greater love hath no man than that a man lay down his life for his friends."

Born in Mansfield Feb. 7, 1900, and growing up here and attending our public schools, there was early instilled in his life an intense love for his country. Upon the organization of the original Seymour Supply Co, which later became the supply company of the 140th Infantry, Clarence volunteered his services and left here Aug. 5 last year for Nevada, Mo., going from there to Camp Doniphan, Okla, and thence overseas as a part of the American Expeditionary Forces, dying Oct. 16 from wounds received in action. Some time after joining the army he transferred to Co. I of the 140th Infantry, of which company he was a member when he died, a telegram officially reporting his death being received by his mother Thursday afternoon.

He is survived by his mother and stepfather, T. J. Slate and wife; five brothers, Elbert, now with the American Expeditionary Forces; Sam of Red Fork, Okla; Burl, Clinton and Clifton of Mansfield, and two sisters, Mrs. S. W. Carter of Mansfield and Mrs. Chas. Howard of St. Louis. One sister, Mrs. Fannie Slate preceded him in death.

Numerous other relatives and hosts of friends also feel their bereavement in the death of Clarence King, who died that liberty and freedom might not perish from the earth." (*Mansfield Mirror* Nov 21, 1918)

Although the body of Pvt. Clarence King arrived in Mansfield August 9, 1921, he was first buried in a communal grave in a French cemetery in Amblaincourt, Meuse. His journey home of nearly three years began on March 21, 1921, when his body was disinterred and transferred to Port Antwerp, Belgium where it was loaded on the ship, *Wheaton*, bound for Hoboken, New Jersey. The final leg of his homeward journey took five days by rail, but he was indeed home at last.

"The remains of Clarence King arrived in Mansfield last Tuesday from France, and was buried Thursday afternoon in the Mansfield Cemetery, being accorded full military honors by the American Legion. Funeral services were held in the C. P. Church Wednesday afternoon, conducted by Revs. L. A. Johnson and J. W. Patterson. Clarence King was a son of Mary Jane King Slate, and enlisted in the service of his country June

27, 1917, and was finally placed in Co. I, 140 Inf., where he came to his death in battle in the Argonne Forest fight. He was struck in the head by fragments of a high explosive shell, September 18, 1918, and died in a hospital in France. Clarence King was barely past 17 years of age when he enlisted in the army. The Mansfield American Legion post was named for him, as he was the first boy from Mansfield to lose his life in battle in the World War." (*Mansfield Mirror* August 11, 1921)

Clarence King's mother, Mary Jane Slate, beside his grave site in the Mansfield Cemetery

Funeral card

MILITARY ABBREVIATIONS

AEF: American Expeditionary Forces

AFC: Army Field Clerk

APO: Army Post Office

ART: Artillery

BKS: Barracks

BN: Battalion

BTRY: Battery

CAC: Coast Artillery Corps

DEP BRIG: Depot Brigade

FA: Field Artillery

FANA: Field Artillery National Army

HA: Horse Artillery

HFC: Horseshoer First Class

HvA: Heavy Artillery

HQ: Head Quarters

INF: Infantry

KIA: Killed in Action

MG BN: Machine Gun Battalion

MOTC: Military Operations Training Course

MTC: Motor Transport Corps

NA: National Army

NG: National Guard

REG: Regiment

RC: Reserve Corps

SAR: Search and Rescue

WFC: Wagoner First Class

MILITARY BIOGRAPHIES

HOMER JOHN AKERS, SR., PVT., US MARINE CORPS (Younger brother of Walter Akers)

Born 5-15-1894 – Died 12-12-1956

He was buried in Thomas Cemetery in Norwood, MO. The inscription on his tombstone reads "PVT US MARINE." He was the son of Granville Akers and Leona Rossetta (Duncan) Akers and was married to Grace Jewell Akers. (findagrave.com)

According to his World War I Draft Registration card, he was 6 feet tall, weighed 200 lbs., and had blue eyes, brown hair, and a ruddy complexion. (www.ancestry.com)

He was inducted at Joplin, MO on 6-21-1917 and served with Port Royal 96, 6th Quantico, VA before going to France on 2-08-1918 with REPL 30 to 5-30-1918 and with the 96th Co. to 8-24-1918. He served overseas from 2-08-1918 to 9-20-1919. He was wounded in action on 7-19-1918 and was in the hospital until 10-03-1918, with the 96th Co. on 1-05-1919, with Co. E, COMP REG on 5-02-1919, and with BKS DET on 10-17-1919. (Missouri Digital Heritage)

A description of the Marine Corps Addenda Roster states that Homer was in the hospital with flu during the 80th and 96th's first campaign at Belleau Wood in June 1918. He was injured by gunshot on 7-20-1918 during the Soissons/Chateau Thierry battle and then again on 10-04-1918 during the Battle of Blanc Mont Ridge. (findagrave.com)

He departed for home from Brest, France on 9-21-1919 aboard the *Von Steuben* and arrived in Hoboken, New Jersey. He later became a rural mail carrier. (www.ancestry.com)

WALTER JACKSON AKERS, PVT., US ARMY/MARINE, (POW) (Older brother of Homer Akers)

Born 8-15-1891 – Died 4-04-1924

He was buried at Oak Forest Cemetery in Douglas County, MO. He was the son of Granville Akers and Leona Rosetta (Duncan) Akers and was married to Nora (Strunk) Damuth. (findagrave.com)

He served with Co. L, 9th Infantry. (MOGenweb.com)

He departed from Hoboken, New Jersey on 8-22-1918 aboard the *Rijndam*. On 1-31-1919, he departed for home from St. Nazaire, France aboard the *Finland* and arrived in Hoboken, New Jersey on 2-14-1919. (www.ancestry.com)

JOHN BENTON "JACK" ALSUP, PVT., US ARMY/MARINE/NATIONAL GUARD

Born 4-02-1890 – Died 10-07-1918

He was buried in Henderson Cemetery in Douglas County, MO. The inscription on his tombstone reads "Missouri Pvt. 70 Inf. 10 Div. 10-7-1918." He was the son of John Lock Alsup and Cynthia A. (Burris) Alsup. (findagrave.com)

According to his World War I Draft Registration card, he was slender, short, and had brown eyes and brown hair. (www.ancestry.com)

He was inducted at Ava, MO on 7-25-1918 and served with Co. 21, 164th DEP BRIG to 8-10-1918 and with Co. A, 70th Infantry until his death. He died of lobar pneumonia; his father, John Alsup of Bertha, MO, was notified of his death. (Missouri Digital Heritage)

OVA "OVIE" ELIJAH BAKER, PVT., US ARMY

Born 3-28-1896 – Died 8-18-1921

He was buried in Baker Cemetery in Wright County, MO. The inscription on his tombstone reads "PVT 3rd Col BN 164 Depot Brigade." He was the son of Thomas Reed Baker, Sr. and Parthena (Stacy) Baker. (findagrave.com)

He was inducted at Hartville, MO on 7-25-1918 and served with the 164th DEP BRIG to 8-10-1918, with HQ DET 210th ENG to 10-12-1918, and with the 210th ENGRS until his discharge. (Missouri Digital Heritage)

CHARLES "CHARLIE" AUSTIN BALL, PVT., US ARMY (Older brother of Palmer French Ball)

Born 8-29-1891 – Died 10-29-1918 in France

He was buried at Lone Star Cemetery in Mountain Grove, MO. He was the son of Estil Alonzo Ball and Elizabeth R. (Poteet) Ball and was married to Rozella "Zella" Wood (Cooper) Ball. The inscription on his tombstone reads "BALL BROTHERS - French 1896-1918, Charlie 1891-1918, 89th DIV in the A.E.F." (findagrave.com)

According to his World War I Draft Registration card, he was of medium height and build and had red hair and blue eyes. (www.ancestry.com)

He was inducted in Ava, MO on 4-26-1918 and departed from New York on 6-04-1918 aboard the *Berrima*. He served with Co. 19, 164th DEP BRIG to 5-15-1918 and with Co. C, 354th Infantry, 89th Division, National Army until his death. He served overseas from 6-04-1918 to 10-27-1918. He died from wounds received in action; his father, Estil Ball of Mountain Grove, MO, was notified of his death. (Missouri Digital Heritage)

He was transported home on 2-22-1919 from Brest, France aboard the *Aquitania* and arrived in New York on 2-28-1919. (www.ancestry.com)

He was awarded the Purple Heart and the World War I Victory Medal. (HonorStates.org)

PALMER FRENCH BALL, PVT., US ARMY (Younger brother of Charlie Austin Ball)

Born 1-27-1896 – Died 11-2-1918 in France

He was buried at Lone Star Cemetery in Mountain Grove, MO. He was the son of Estil Alonzo Ball and Elizabeth R. (Poteet) Ball. The inscription on his tombstone reads "BALL BROTHERS - French 1896-1918, Charlie 1891-1918, 89th DIV in the A.E.F." (findagrave.com)

He was inducted at Ava, MO on 4-26-1918 and served with Co. 19, 164th DEP BRIG from 4-28-1918 to 5-15-1918 and with Co. G, 354th Infantry Item Co., 89th Division, NA to 11-02-1918. He died from wounds received in action; his father, Estil Ball, was notified of his death. (Missouri Digital Heritage)

On 6-5-1918, he departed from Montreal, Canada aboard the *Ascanius*. On 8-06-1921, he was transported home from Antwerp, Belgium aboard the *Wheaton* and arrived at Hoboken, New Jersey. According to his World War I Draft Registration card, he was of medium height and build and had light brown hair and gray eyes. (www.ancestry.com)

He was awarded the Purple Heart and the World War I Victory Medal. (HonorStates.org)

ROY WESLEY BARE, PVT., US ARMY

Born 12-8-1889 in Wright County – Died 10-13-1919 in France

He died of disease and was buried at Friendship Cemetery in Mountain Grove, Missouri. He was the son of John Henry Bare and Naomi J. Bare. (findagrave.com)

He was inducted in Hartville, MO on 5-28-1918. (Missouri Digital Heritage)

He departed from Philadelphia, PA on 8-14-1918 aboard the *Rhesus*. He was a member of Co. C, 339th MG BN. He was transported home on 5-01-1921 from Cherbourg, France aboard the *Wheaton* and arrived in Hoboken, New Jersey. According to his World War I Draft Registration card, he was tall, of medium build, and had dark brown hair and blue eyes. (www.ancestry.com)

He died of broncho pneumonia; his father, John Bare of Mountain Grove, MO, was notified of his death. (Missouri Digital Heritage)

He was awarded the Purple Heart and the World War I Victory Medal. (HonorStates.org)

OREAN HARVEY BASS, PVT. 1st CLASS, US ARMY/MARINE

Born 1-02-1897 – Died 2-23-1952

He was buried at Ashley Cemetery in Wright County, MO. He was the son of William Nelson Bass and Violetta Evangeline (Graham) Bass and was married to Dora Edna (Felkner) Bass. (findagrave.com)

He enlisted on 3-26-1917 in Iola, KS. He departed from New York on 5-19-1918 aboard the *Briton*. (www.ancestry.com)

He served with Co. B, 110th Field Signal Battalion, 35th Division, Kansas Signal Corps. He trained at Fort Sill, Camp Doniphan, OK. His engagements included Vosges Sector, France; St. Mihiel Offensive; Argonne-Meuse Offensive; and Verdun Front. He was awarded 2 War Service Chevrons for 1 year overseas. (Missouri Digital Heritage)

His rank was Private First Class; he was discharged on 5-19-1919 at Camp Funston, KS. (Clarence King Post American Legion's *Service Record Book*)

JAMES JOHN BAUSCH, US ARMY/MARINE

Born 7-23-1892 – Died 4-26-1987

He was buried in Shady Grove Cemetery in Aldrich, MO. He was the son of Michael H. Bausch and Katharina (Custer) Bausch. He was married to Bertha Ann (Newton) Bausch who died the day after giving birth to their son. He later married Freda O. (Griffin) Bausch. (findagrave.com)

He departed from New York on 8-09-1917 aboard the *Saxonia* and served with Co. C, 19th Engineers (Railway). According to his World War I Draft Registration card, he was of medium height and build and had dark brown hair and dark brown eyes. His residence was listed as Wright County, MO. (www.ancestry.com)

CHARLES WALTER BEACH, PVT., US ARMY

Born 7-15-1887 – Died 7-11-1978

He was buried in the Springfield National Cemetery in Greene County, MO. He was the son of Charles Leonard Beach and Lura Elizabeth (Alverson) Beach and was married to Virginia Sue "Bobby" Beach. (findagrave.com)

He was inducted at Hartville, MO on 5-28-1918 and served with 163 DEP BRIG to 6-14-1918 and with HQ Co., 350th Infantry until his discharge on 6-15-1920. He served overseas from 8-11-1918 to 5-31-1919. (Missouri Digital Heritage)

He departed from Brooklyn, New York on 8-11-1918 aboard the *Delta*. According to his World War I Draft Registration card, he was slender, 5 ft 8 in tall, and had brown hair and brown eyes. (www.ancestry.com)

FRANK BECKETT, PVT., US ARMY

Born 10-10-1888 - Died 10-06-1918 in France

He was buried in Pea Ridge Cemetery in Wright County, MO. He was the son of Thomas H. Beckett and Sarah Elizabeth Beckett and was married to Viva E. King. (findagrave.com)

According to his World War I Draft Registration card, he was tall and slender and had brown hair and gray eyes. He departed from New York on 6-04-1918 aboard the *Caronia*. He was a private in Co. H, 356th Infantry, 89th Division. (www.ancestry.com)

He was inducted at Rockport, MO on 10-02-1917. He served overseas from 6-04-1918 to 10-06-1918. He was killed in action; his wife, Viva Beckett of Hamburg, IA, was notified of his death. (Missouri Digital Heritage)

He was awarded the Purple Heart. (HonorStates.org)

MAURICE S. BERRY, US ARMY/MARINE

Born 9-17-1895 – Died 7-05-1928

He was born in Pleasant Valley, Wright County, Mo. He was buried at Olive Branch Cemetery in Portsmouth, VA. He was the son of Robert Duff Berry and Louisa Carver Berry and was married to Anna Martha (Wolfe) Justice. (findagrave.com)

He was inducted in Kansas City, MO on 8-09-1915 and served on the *USS Arizona* to 4-06-1917 and in Norfolk, VA to 4-14-1918. (Missouri Digital Heritage)

HENRY OTTO F. BINKLEY, PVT., US ARMY

Born 1-28-1887 – Died 10-15-1918 in France

He died from wounds and was buried in St. Mihiel American Cemetery in Thiaucourt, France. The inscription on his tombstone reads "PVT. 129 FIELD ART. 35 DIV. MISSOURI." He was the son of John Binkley and Clemence J. Binkley. He was married to Bessie Ward on 6-26-1915. (findagrave.com)

He was inducted in Kansas City, MO on 8-16-1917. He departed from New York on 5-27-1918 aboard the *Khiva* and was a member of Battery F, 129th Field Artillery Regiment, 35th Division. (www.ancestry.com)

He served overseas from 5-27-1918 to 10-15-1918. He died from wounds received in action; his father, John Binkley, of Hartville, MO was notified of his death. (Missouri Digital Heritage)

According to his World War I Draft Registration card, he was of medium height and build and had black hair and light blue eyes. (www.ancestry.com)

He was awarded the Purple Heart and the World War I Victory Medal. (HonorStates.org)

SHERMAN WINFIELD BORDERS, WAG., US ARMY/MARINE

Born 9-26-1891 – Died 7-19-1969

He was buried in the Seymour Masonic Cemetery in Webster County, MO. He was the son of Levi T. Borders and Ursula Ann (Floyd) Borders. He was married to Opal Leona (Cummins) Borders. (findagrave.com)

He departed from Hoboken, New Jersey on 5-02-1918 aboard the *Great Northern* and became a private with Co. F, 110th Regiment Engineers. (www.ancestry.com)

He was inducted at Hartville, MO on 10-2-1917. He served with 164th DEP BRIG to 10-22-1917 and with Co. F, 110th Engineers until his discharge. He served as a wagoner overseas from 5-2-1918 to 4-19-1919. (Missouri Digital Heritage)

HARLEY WILLIAM BRAGG, PVT., US ARMY/NATIONAL GUARD

Born 3-13-1898 – Died 6-21-1918 in France

He died in Gerardmer, Departement des Vosges, Lorraine, France, and was buried in the Meuse-Argonne American Cemetery in Romagne, France. The inscription on his tombstone reads "PVT. 139 INF. 35 DIV. MISSOURI." He was the son of William Oliver Bragg and Mary Ann (Newman) Bragg. (findagrave.com)

He was inducted at Tarkio, MO on 6-02-1917. He departed from New York on 4-25-1918 aboard the *Caronia*. (www.ancestry.com)

As a private, he served with Co. A, 139th Infantry Regiment, 35th Division. He served overseas from 4-25-1918 to 6-21-1918. He died of peritonsillar abscess; his father, William Bragg, of Cedar Gap, MO was notified of his death. (Missouri Digital Heritage)

He was awarded the World War I Victory Medal. (HonorStates.org)

JAMES MARION BRANSTETTER, PVT., US ARMY/MARINE

Born 5-27-1894 – Died 11-28-1918

He was buried in the New Hope Cemetery in Hartville, MO. He was the son of Michael Branstetter and Laura (Little) Branstetter. (findagrave.com)

He was inducted at Hartville, MO on 7-25-1918 and served with 164th DEP BRIG to 8-10-1918 and with BTRY E, 29th Field Artillery until his death. He died of broncho pneumonia; Mrs. Elsia Branstetter of Hartville, MO was notified of his death. (Missouri Digital Heritage)

According to his World War I Draft Registration card, he was tall, of medium build, and had black hair and black eyes. (www.ancestry.com)

WILLIAM "WILLIE" HENRY BRASHER

Born 11-28-1887 Mansfield, MO – Died 5-11-1968

He was buried at White Chapel Memorial Gardens in Springfield, MO. He was the son of William Alexander Brasher and Sarah Margaret (Pool) Brasher and was married to Stella Mae (Newton) Brasher. (findagrave.com)

According to his World War I Draft Registration card, he was of medium height and build and had dark brown hair and gray eyes. (www.ancestry.com)

JESSE BRAZEAL, CPL., US ARMY/MARINE

Born 2-6-1895 – Died 11-18-1918

He was buried in Wolf Creek Primitive Baptist Cemetery in Wright County, MO. He was the son of James Henderson Brazeal and Mary Emaline (Moore) Brazeal. (findagrave.com)

According to his World War I Draft Registration card, he was tall, of medium build, and had red hair and blue eyes. (www.ancestry.com)

He was inducted at Hartville, MO on 7-25-1918. He served with the 164th DEP BRIG to 8-10-1918 and with BTRY E, 29th Field Artillery until his death. He died of pneumonia; his father, James Brazeal, of Mansfield, MO was notified of his death. (Missouri Digital Heritage)

FLOYD DANIEL BRECKNER, PVT., US ARMY/MARINE

Born 5-22-1894 – Died 11-25-1917

He was buried in Pleasant Mound Cemetery in Douglas County, MO. The inscription on his tombstone reads "Our Soldier Boy." He was the son of August Adam Breckner and Laura Belle (Hamilton) Breckner. (findagrave.com)

According to his World War I Draft Registration card, he was slender, tall, and had brown hair and brown eyes. (www.ancestry.com)

He was inducted at Ava, MO on 9-18-1917 and served with BTRY C, 342nd Field Artillery and with the 110 AM TN, Co. D until his death. He died of lobar pneumonia; his mother, Belle Breckner, of Sedan, MO was notified of his death. (Missouri Digital Heritage)

FRANKLIN OLIVER BRIGGS, COOK, US ARMY/MARINE

Born 10-20-1895 – Died 4-11-1961

He was buried in the Ava Cemetery in Ava, MO. He was the son of James Oliver Briggs and Dicy Ketura Briggs and was married to Opal E. (Fletcher) Briggs. (findagrave.com)

He was inducted at Ava, MO on 6-27-1917 and served with Supply Co. 6, MO Infantry MG and Supply Co., 140th Infantry until his discharge. He served overseas from 4-25-1918 to 4-28-1919. (Missouri Digital Heritage)

He departed from Brooklyn, New York on 4-25-1918 aboard the *Shropshire*. He was a cook in Supply Co., 140th Infantry, 35th Division. He departed for home on 4-15-1919 from St. Nazaire, France aboard the *Nansemond*. (www.ancestry.com)

JOSEPH HILLARY BROPHY, CPL., US ARMY/MARINE

Born 11-12-1888 – Died 4-20-1980

He was buried in Seymour Masonic Cemetery in Seymour, MO. He was the son of Patrick Charles Brophy and Mary Ann Brophy and was married to Callie Jane (Tucker) Brophy. (findagrave.com)

He was inducted at Houston, MO on 6-24-1918 at 29 7/12 years of age, and served the 162nd DEP BRIG to 7-25-1918. He served overseas from 9-08-1918 to 7-23-1919. He served with ADM Labor Co., 163 Army SERV C to 11-20-1918 and with ADM Labor Co. 12, ASC ADV ORD DEP 4 to 2-05-1919. (Missouri Digital Heritage)

He departed for home on 9-08-1918 as a member of Squad No. 16 with the 3rd Administrative Labor Co.

According to his World War I Draft Registration card, he was slender, of medium height, and had black hair and light brown eyes. (www.ancestry.com)

CHARLES A. BROWN, PVT., US ARMY

Born 12-23-1888– Died 11-16-1918 in France

He died from disease and was buried in the Meuse-Argonne American Cemetery in Romagne, France. He belonged to the 27th Engineer Regiment. He was awarded the World War I Victory Medal. (HonorStates.org)

According to his World War I Draft Registration card, he was tall, stout, and had brown hair and brown eyes. He resided in Norwood, MO. (www.ancestry.com)

HENRY OSCAR BROWN, COOK, US ARMY/MARINE

Born 2-25-1896 – Died 11-13-1955

He was buried in the Mansfield Cemetery. He was the son of Daniel R. "Bud" Brown and Marinda Etta "Minnie" (Wendt) Brown and was married to Ruth Beatrice (Turner) Brown. (findagrave.com)

He was inducted in Marshfield, MO on 10-3-1917 and served with 15 Co., 164th DEP BRIG to 10-05-1917, with BTRY D, 341st Field Artillery to 2-12-1918, and Casual to 3-03-1918. He served overseas from 3-06-1918 to 7-27-1919. After he was injured on 8-29-1918, he was at CP Funston AUT REPL Draft to 3-23-1918 and CLASS CP 1st DEP DIV to 4-18-1918. (Missouri Digital Heritage)

He served with Co. G, 125th Infantry, 32nd Division. He trained at Camp Funston, Kansas; Staegn, France. He was awarded the Purple Heart, Oak Leaf, Three Battle Stars, and the Presidential Citation and was discharged on 8-2-1919. (Clarence King Post American Legion's *Service Record Book*)

According to his World War I Draft Registration card, he was 5'9", 190 lbs., and had black hair, brown eyes, and a dark complexion. (www.ancestry.com)

IRA CHELSEA BROWN, PVT., US ARMY/MARINES

Born 5-23-1896 – Died 10-01-1918 in France

He was buried in Highland Cemetery in Iola, KS. He was the son of James Marion Brown and Rue Alice (Lumpkins) Brown. He served with Co. L2, KS Infantry, Co. B3, KS Infantry, and Co. B, 139th Infantry. (findagrave.com)

He was living in Norwood, MO in Wright County when he departed from New York on 4-25-1918 aboard the *Coronia*. (www.ancestry.com)

He was killed in action and was awarded the Purple Heart and the World War I Victory Medal. (HonorStates.org)

JAMES MADISON BROWN, PVT., US ARMY/MARINE

Born 1-01-1896 - Died 10-18-1918

He was buried in Fannon Cemetery in Douglas County. He was the son of James Brown and Lizzie T. (Thomas) Brown. (findagrave.com)

He was inducted at Ava, MO on 7-25-1918 and served with BTRY B, 29th Field Artillery until his death. He died of pneumonia at Camp Funston, KS on 10-18-1918; his father, James Brown of Squires, MO, was notified of his death. (Missouri Digital Heritage)

According to his World War I Draft Registration card, he was of medium height and build and had light-colored hair and blue eyes. (www.ancestry.com)

DELBERT BURKS (BURK), PVT., US ARMY

Born 4-20-1893– Died 10-04-1918 in France

He was the son of Samuel Allen Burks and Mary Elizabeth Burks. He resided in Prior, Douglas County, MO.
He was buried in the Meuse-Argonne American Cemetery in Romagne, France. The inscription on his tombstone reads "PVT. 2 SANITARY TRAIN 2 DIV. MISSOURI." (findagrave.com)

He served with the 2nd Division, 2nd Sanitary Trains. He was awarded the Purple Heart and the World War I Victory Medal. (HonorStates.org)

He was killed in action; his father, Samuel Burks of Prior, MO, was notified of his death. (Missouri Digital Heritage)

According to his World War I Draft Registration card, he was of medium build and height and had dark brown hair and dark brown eyes. (www.ancestry.com)

JOHN WILLIAM CANIFAX, WAG., US ARMY/MARINE

Born 4-24-1895 – Died 7-18-1964

He was buried at Spring Creek Cemetery, Douglas County, MO. (findagrave.com)

He was inducted at Ava, MO on 9-18-1917 and served as a wagoner with Battery C, 342nd Field Artillery. He was overseas from 6-28-1918 to 5-27-1919. (Missouri Digital Heritage)

According to his World War I Draft Registration card, he was of medium build and height and had auburn hair and light brown eyes. (www.ancestry.com)

RAYMOND CARRICK, PFC., US ARMY/MARINE/NATIONAL GUARD

Born 10-18-1896 – Died 12-14-1983

He was buried in Maryland Veterans Cemetery in Fort Washington, Maryland. He was the son of James Skeen Carrick, Sr. and Nancy Mason (Upchurch) Carrick and was married to Effie Jane (Phillips) Carrick. (findagrave.com)

He was inducted at Seymour, MO on 6-27-1917 and served with Supply Co., 6th Infantry MO NG Supply Co., 140th Infantry. He served overseas from 4-25-1918 to 4-28-1919. (Missouri Digital Heritage)

According to his World War I Draft Registration card, he was 5'7", 142 lbs., and had brown hair and blue eyes. (www.ancestry.com)

CHARLES THOMAS CARTER, PVT., US ARMY

Born 3-08-1892 – Died 9-27-1920

He was buried in Mount Pisgah Cemetery in Texas County, MO. He was the son of Thomas Benton Carter and Mary Ann (Pitman) Carter. (findagrave.com)

He was inducted at Houston, MO on 4-26-1918 and served with Co. 38, 164th DEP BRIG to 5-15-1918 and with Co. I, 356th Infantry until his discharge. He served overseas from 6-04-1918 to 3-18-1919. He suffered undetermined injuries on 10-06-1918 and received 100% disability. (Missouri Digital Heritage)

He served as a private in Camp Dodge, No. 3 Detachment of the 160th Infantry. He departed for home from Bordeaux, France on 3-6-1919 aboard the *Walter A. Luckenbach* and arrived in Hoboken, New Jersey on 3-19-1919. According to his World War I Draft Registration card, he was single, slender, short, and had light-colored hair and blue eyes. (www.ancestry.com)

He died of an accident and was awarded the World War I Victory Medal. (HonorStates.org)

GARRETT WILLIAM "CHINA" CARTER, SGT., US ARMY/MARINE (Younger brother of John Alva Carter)

Born 5-30-1899 – Died 7-04-1959

He was buried in the Mansfield Cemetery. He was the son of John Henry Carter and Suzanne Isabelle (Caskey) Carter. He was married to Blanche Catherine (Davis) Carter. (findagrave.com)

W.F.C. Garrett Carter enlisted in April 1917. He trained at Fort Sill, OK and embarked for overseas in May 1918. His engagements included the St. Mihiel, Meuse-Argonne, and

Verdun Battles. He returned to the United States in April 1919 and was discharged in May 1919. (Clarence King Post American Legion's *Service Record Book*)

He was inducted on 6-27-1917 at Mansfield, MO and served as a wagoner with Supply Co., 6th Infantry MO NG and Supply Co., 140th Infantry, 35th Division until his discharge. He served overseas from 4-25-1918 to 4-28-1919. (Missouri Digital Heritage)

He departed from Brooklyn, NY aboard the *Shropshire* on 4-25-1918 as a Pvt. Following the Armistice, he departed for home from St. Nazaire, France on 4-15-1919 aboard the *Nansemond*. (www.ancestry.com)

JOHN "BULL" ALVA CARTER, HFC, US ARMY/ MARINE (Older brother of Garrett Carter)

Born 2-05-1895 – Died 11-19-1969

He was buried in the Mansfield Cemetery. He was the son of John Henry Carter and Suzanne Isabelle (Caskey) Carter. He was married to Airy Eva Josephine (Brown) Carter. (findagrave.com)

He was inducted at Mansfield, MO on 6-27-1917 and served as a horseshoer with Supply Co., 6th Infantry MO NG. He was overseas from 4-25-1918 to 5-27-1919. (Missouri Digital Heritage)

H.F.C. John Carter enlisted in April 1917 and served with Supply Co., 140th Infantry, 35th Division. He trained at Fort Sill, OK and embarked in May 1918. His engagements included the St. Mihiel, Meuse-Argonne, and Verdun Battles. He returned to the United States in April 1919 and was discharged in May 1919. (Clarence King Post American Legion's *Service Record Book*)

According to his World War I Draft Registration card, he was 5'8", 160 lbs. with brown hair, blue eyes, and a ruddy complexion. (www.ancestry.com)

JAMES C. CHADWELL, PVT., US ARMY

Born 8-08-1894 – Died 10-26-1918 in France

He died in Bougnon, France and was buried in Denlow Cemetery in Douglas County, MO. He was the son of Peter and Octavia Chadwell. (findagrave.com)

According to his World War I Draft Registration card, he was single, of medium height and build, and had black hair and blue eyes. He departed from New York on 8-15-1918 aboard the *Kashmir*. (www.ancestry.com)

He was inducted at Ava, MO on 5-28-1918 and served with the 163rd DEP BRIG from 5-28-1918 to 6-14-1918 and with Co. G, 350th Infantry, 88th Division to 10-28-1918. He served overseas from 8-15-1918 to 10-26-1918. He died of pneumonia; his mother, Mrs. Octavia Coffman of Cold Springs, MO, was notified of his death. (Missouri Digital Heritage)

He was awarded the World War I Victory Medal. (HonorStates.org)

RALPH HOYT CHAPMAN, US ARMY/ MARINE/NATIONAL GUARD

Born 9-02-1881 - Died 11-04-1956

He was buried at Number Five Cemetery, Wright County, MO. He was the son of Calvin Morgan Chapman and Eliza Madera (Bryan) Chapman. He was married to Clella Clementine (Newton) Chapman and later to Ida M. Peacock (Morris) Chapman. He was the County Surveyor for many years. (findagrave.com)

He was inducted at Hartville, MO on 10/02/1917. He served as a wagoner with the 164th DEP BRIG to 10-22-1917 and with Co. F, 110th ENGRS until his discharge. He served overseas from 5-02-1918 to 4-19-1919. (Missouri Digital Heritage)

According to his World War I Draft Registration card, he was of medium height and build and had brown hair and gray eyes. (www.ancestry.com)

ALEXANDER CLARK, CPL., US ARMY

Born 6-12-1895 – Died 10-07-1918 in Brest, France

He was buried in Little Creek Cemetery in Hartville, Missouri. The inscription on his tombstone reads "PVT MED REP UNIT NO 21." He was the son of James Clark and Elizabeth (Kelley) Clark. (findagrave.com)

He was inducted at Hartville, MO on 7-05-1918 and served with Co. H, 11th REPL & TNG BN Camp McArthur from 7-09-1918 to 8-30-1918 and with the MED REPL UNIT 21 until his death. He served overseas from 9-15-1918 to 10-07-1918. He died of bronchial pneumonia; his father, James Clark, of Hartville, MO was notified of his death. (Missouri Digital Heritage)

He departed from Hoboken, New Jersey, on 9-15-1918 aboard the *Pocahontas.* According to his World War I Draft Registration card, he was single, of medium height and build, and had dark hair and gray eyes. (www.ancestry.com)

He was awarded the World War I Victory Medal. (HonorStates.org)

CLAUDE NOBLE CLARK, PVT., US ARMY/MARINE

Born 7-22-1894 – Died 4-16-1970

He was buried in the Mansfield Cemetery in Mansfield, MO. He was the son of John Wesley Clark and Nellie T. (Jenkins) Clark and was married to Pearl Clark. (findagrave.com)

He enlisted at Warsaw, MO on 7-21-1918 and served with the 164th DEP BRIG to 8-21-1918 and with the 105th SN TN until his discharge. (Missouri Digital Heritage)

He departed from Hoboken, New Jersey on 9-08-1918 aboard the *Desna*. He was a private in the Exceptional Medical Replacement Draft, Unit No. 34 and the Camp Funston Detachment 105th Sanitary Train, 30th Division. (www.ancestry.com)

He departed for home on 3-21-1919 from St. Nazaire, France aboard the *Huron* and was discharged on 4-14-1919. According to his World War I Draft Registration card, he was of medium height and build and had light brown hair and grey eyes. (www.ancestry.com)

HOWARD NOAH CLAXTON, WAG., US ARMY

Born 11-8-1894 – Died 7-27-1977

He was buried at Steele Memorial Cemetery, Hartville, MO. He was the son of Ella Claxton. He was married to Hetty (Graven) Claxton. (findagrave.com)

He was inducted at Seymour, MO on 6-27-1917 at age 22 and served as a wagoner with Supply Co., 6th Infantry MO NG and with Supply Co., 140th Infantry, 35th Division. He served overseas from 4-25-1918 to 4-15-1919. (Missouri Digital Heritage)

He departed from Brooklyn, NY aboard the *Shropshire* on 4-25-1918. He returned to the U.S. aboard the *Nansemond* from St. Nazaire, France on 4-15-1919. According to his World War I Draft Registration card, he was of medium height and build and had brown hair and gray eyes. (www.ancestry.com)

He was involved in the Occupation of Fecht Sector, the Meuse-Argonne Offensive, and the Occupation of Verdun Sector. He was discharged on 5-13-1919. (Clarence King Post American Legion's *Service Record Book*)

JAMES "TINY" ANDERSON CLAXTON, PVT., US ARMY/MARINE

Born: 7-06-1894 – Died 8-13-1960

He was buried in Claxton Cemetery in Hartville, MO. He was the son of Edward Anderson Claxton and Ella Susan (Bolian) Claxton and was married to Lillian Frances (Davis) Claxton. He was inducted at Hartville, MO on 10-02-1917 and served with Co. 7, 164th DEP BRIG to 10-22-1917 and with Co. F, 110th ENGRS until his discharge. (Missouri Digital Heritage)

According to his World War I Draft Registration card, he was of medium height, stout, and had light brown hair and blue eyes. (familysearch.org)

BERLIN FINIS CODAY, PVT., US ARMY

Born 5-15-1897 – Died 4-21-1966

He was buried in Mount Olivet Cemetery, Salt Lake City, Utah. He was the son of Thomas Coday and Luello Doreen (Johnson) Coday. He was married to Ruby C. (Latimer) Coday. (findagrave.com)

He was inducted at Hartville, MO on 8-14-1918 and served with Co. 11, Rahes Auto & Tractor School, Kansas City, MO to 10-13-1918 and with the 156 Depot Brigade as a private until his discharge. (Missouri Digital Heritage)

According to his World War I Draft Registration card, he was of medium height and build and had black hair and black eyes. (www.ancestry.com)

WALTER CLAY CODAY, SGT., US ARMY/MARINE/NATIONAL GUARD

Born 11-13-1890 – Died 1-20-1961

He was buried in the Mansfield Cemetery in Mansfield, MO. He was the son of Henry Coday and Elizabeth Lucinda (Chapman) Coday and was married to Opal (Freeman) Coday. (findagrave.com)

He was inducted at Mansfield, MO on 6-27-1917 and served as a wagoner with the Supply Co., 6th Infantry MO NG and Supply Co., 140th Infantry. He served overseas from 4-25-1918 to 4-28-1919. (Missouri Digital Heritage)

He departed for home from St. Nazaire, France on 4-15-1919 aboard the *Nansemond*. According to his World War I Draft Registration card, he was married, of medium height and build, and had light-colored hair and light blue eyes. (www.ancestry.com)

MONROE WILLIAM COLLINS, PVT., US ARMY/MARINE

Born 2-14-1895 - Died 10-09-1918

He was buried in Carroll Cemetery in Howell County, MO. He was the son of Samuel Milton Collins and Rushia Belle Collins. (findagrave.com) He was inducted at Ava, MO on 7-25-1918 and served with Co. 21, 164th DEP BRIG to 8-10-1918 and with Co. A, 70th Infantry until his death. He died of lobar pneumonia on 10-09-1918; his father, Samuel Collins of Minard, MO, was notified of his death. (Missouri Digital Heritage)

WILLIE M. CORNETT, PVT., US ARMY/MARINE

Born 1-22-1895 – Died 12-28-1917

He was buried in Stamper Cemetery in Douglas County, MO. He was the son of Esquire S. "Squire" Cornett and Emily Ritta (Dixon) Essary. (findagrave.com)

He was inducted at Ava, MO on 9-18-1917 and served with BTRY C, 342nd Field Artillery until his death. He died of broncho pneumonia on 12-28-1917; his mother, Mrs. E. R. Cornett of Rome, MO, was notified of his death. (Missouri Digital Heritage)

WILLIAM GLEN CRAIG, WAG., US ARMY

Born 5-15-1895 – Died 2-09-1957

He was buried in the Mansfield Cemetery. He was the son of John Nelson Craig and Elizabeth "Lizzie" (Ranft) Craig and was married to Oma (Freeman) Craig. (findagrave.com)

He was inducted at Mansfield on 6-27-1917 at 22 ½ years of age and served as a wagoner with the Missouri Supply Co., 6th Infantry and with Supply Co., 140th Infantry, 35th Division. He served overseas from 4-25-1918 to 4-28-1919. (Missouri Digital Heritage)

According to his World War I Draft Registration card, he was 5'6", 165 lbs., bald, with hazel eyes and light complexion. (www.ancestry.com)

W.F.C. William Craig enlisted in April 1917. He trained at Fort Sill, OK and embarked in May 1918. His engagements included the St. Mihiel, Meuse-Argonne, and Verdun Battles. He returned to the United States in April 1919 and was discharged in May 1919. (Clarence King Post American Legion's *Service Record Book)*

EARNIE NICHOLAS CRIPPEN, PVT., US ARMY/MARINE

Born 7-27-1896 – Died 8-01-1977 in Joshua Tree, San Bernadino County, CA.

He was buried at Loma Vista Memorial Park. He was the son of William Loranzo Crippen and Lular Jane (Dean) Crippen and was married to Gertie May (Stout) Crippen. (findagrave.com)

He was inducted at Hartville, MO on 8-27-1918 and served with Co. B, 28th MG BN (Machine Gun Battalion). (Missouri Digital Heritage)

According to his World War I Draft Registration card, he was of medium height, stout, and had black hair and brown eyes. (www.ancestry.com)

JESS S. CRISP, PVT., US ARMY/MARINE

Born 4-05-1894 in Manes, MO – Died 9-28-1918 in France

Although erroneously reported to his family as missing in action, he was killed in action and died in Charpentry, Departement de la Meuse, Lorraine, France and was buried in the Meuse-Argonne American Cemetery and Memorial in Romagne, France. He was the son of Mary Jane (Crisp) Blankenship and the stepson of Andrew J. Blankenship. (findagrave.com)

He entered the service from Kansas and belonged to Co. A, 129th Machine Gun Battalion, 35th Division. He was also in the National Guard. (findagrave.com)

According to his World War I Draft Registration card, he was of medium height and build and had light-colored hair and blue eyes. (www.ancestry.com)

He was awarded the Purple Heart. (HonorStates.org)

JAMES B. CROUCH, US NAVY

Born 6-28-1892 – Died 3-01-1974

He was buried in the Mansfield Cemetery in Mansfield, MO. He was married to Lockie Ovene (Craig) Crouch.

"J. B. Crouch of Fort Wayne, Indiana renewed his subscription. 'Will let you know when and where to change my address when I go back to the Navy.' He had served in the Navy before coming to Mansfield where he acted as band director and assisted in the Mirror Office." (*Mansfield Mirror* June 14, 1917)

WILLIAM "JACK" COLEMAN CURTIS, PVT., US ARMY/MARINE

Born 1-16-1891 – Died 2-13-1974

He was buried in Souder Cemetery in Ozark County, MO. He was the son of John Lawson Curtis and Julia Grace (Reynolds) Curtis and was married to Flora Ann (Leroy) Curtis. (findagrave.com)

He was inducted in Ava, MO on 6-24-1918 at 27 7/12 years of age. He served in Co. B, 153rd Infantry to 9-27-1918 and with Co. E, 51st Infantry until his discharge. He served overseas from 8-06-1918 to 6-12-1919. (Missouri Digital Heritage)

RALPH RAYMOND DAKE, PVT., US ARMY/MARINE

Born 3-22-1894 – Died 9-09-1959 in Los Angeles, CA.

He was buried in West Side District Cemetery, Taft, CA. He was the son of Perry Thomas Dake and Sarah Catherine (Hays) Dake and was married to Etta May (Burgess) Dake. (findagrave.com)

He was inducted at Hartville, MO on 10-2-1917. He served with 7th Co., 164th DEP BRIG and with Co. F, 110th Engineers and was overseas from 5-2-1918 to 4-19-1919. (Missouri Digital Heritage)

LON DAVIDSON, PVT., US ARMY/ MARINE

Born 11-26-1894 – Died 8-04-1964

He was buried in Little Creek Cemetery in Hartville, MO. He was the son of William A. Davidson and Lucy Davidson and was married to Thursa A. (Ely) Davidson. (findagrave.com)

He was inducted at Hartville, MO on 10-02-1917 and served with 164th DEP BRIG to 10-15-1917 and with the 314th Engineer TN until his discharge. He served overseas from 6-12-1918 to 5-23-1919. (Missouri Digital Heritage)

He departed from New York on 6-12-1918 aboard the *Carpathia*. (www.ancestry.com)

He enlisted on 10-02-1917 and became a wagoner, belonging to the unit Wagoner-Demob. Grp. Camp Funston, KS, 314th Eng. Trn., 89th Div. He was discharged on 6-09-1919. (Headstone Applications for Military Veterans)

He departed for home on 5-15-1919 from Brest, France aboard the *Harrisburg* and arrived in Hoboken, New Jersey on 5-23-1919. (www.ancestry.com)

BOB "BOBBIE" DAVIS, PVT., US ARMY/MARINE

Born 4-28-1893 - Died 2-12-1981

He was buried in the Nancy Newton Cemetery in Wright County, MO. He was the son of John Davis and Martha Ann (Rush) Davis, and he was married to Oma Elizabeth "Betty" (Newton) Davis. (findagrave.com)

He was inducted at Hartville on 5-28-1918 and served with the 163rd DEP BRIG to 6-14-1918 and with Co. F, 350th Infantry until his discharge. He was overseas from 8-11-1918 to 5-30-1919. (Missouri Digital Heritage)

He was hospitalized for five months while in France after fighting in a battle in which poisonous gases were used. He departed for home on 5-19-1919 from St. Nazaire, France aboard the *Aeolus* and arrived at Camp Alexander, Newport News, VA. He was discharged on 6-7-1919. In the 1940 census, his occupation was listed as a barber. According to his World War I Draft Registration card, he was of medium height and build, single, with dark hair and gray eyes. (www.ancestry.com)

JESSE ELMER DAVIS, PVT., US ARMY

Born 11-18-1892 – Died 7-31-1980

He was buried in the Steele Memorial Cemetery in Hartville, MO. He was the son of Benjamin Samuel Davis and Marzettia (Reese) Davis. He married Artie Ethel (Moore) Davis on 12-07-1919.

He enlisted on 7-25-1918 and was discharged on 1-26-1919. According to his World War I Draft Registration card, he was of medium height and build and had black hair and gray eyes. (www.ancestry.com)

OREN LINZY DAVIS

Born 9-12-1888 – Died 2-23-1965

He was buried in Seymour Masonic Cemetery in Webster County, MO. He was the son of Linzy Tucker Davis and Nancy Ellen (Cox) Davis and was married to Thelma A. Davis. (findagrave.com)

According to his registration card, he was of medium height and build and had black hair and brown eyes. (www.ancestry.com)

CURTIS KELLY DENNEY, PVT., US ARMY/MARINE

Born 11-10-1885 – Died 10-18-1918

He was buried at Spring Creek Cemetery in Douglas County, MO. He was the son of Charles Winburn Denney and China "Chiney" (Hammons) Denney. (findagrave.com)

He was inducted at Ava, MO on 7-25-1918 and served with Co. 21, 164th DEP BRIG to 8-10-1918 and with HQ 210th Engineers TN until his death. He died of bronchial pneumonia at Camp Funston, KS; his father, Charley Denney, of Oswego, MO was notified of his death. (Missouri Digital Heritage)

According to his World War I Draft Registration card, he was of medium height and build and had dark brown hair and blue eyes. (www.ancestry.com)

FRANK ALVA DENNIS, CPL., US ARMY/MARINE

Born 6-08-1896 – Died 1-25-1981

He was buried in the Mansfield Cemetery in Mansfield, MO. He was the son of William Henry Dennis and Mary Deliah (Hanks) Dennis and was married to Lola Clementine (Gaskill) Dennis. (findagrave.com)

He was inducted at Hartville, MO on 8-27-1918 and served with the 164th DEP BRIG until his discharge. (Missouri Digital Heritage)

MARVIN HANKS DENNIS, PVT., US ARMY/MARINE (Older brother of Ural Dennis)

Born 10-24-1892 - Died 1-19-1981

He was buried in the Mansfield Cemetery. He was the son of Joseph Harrison Dennis and Laura Jane (Hanks) Dennis and was married to Clella Jane (Gaskill) Dennis. (findagrave.com)

He was inducted at Hartville, MO on 10-2-1917 and served with 164th DEP BRIG to 10-22-1917 and with Co. F, 110th Engineers until his discharge. He was overseas from 5-2-1918 to 4-19-1919. (Missouri Digital Heritage)

He departed from Hoboken, New Jersey, aboard the *Great Northern*. According to his World War I Draft Registration card, he was slender and tall and had light-colored hair and blue eyes. (www.ancestry.com)

Per the 1950 Missouri Census he was a mail carrier and farmer.

URAL RAPHAEL DENNIS (Younger brother of Marvin Dennis)

Born 3-13-1898 – Died 1-31-1968

He was buried in the Mansfield Cemetery. He was the son of Joseph Harrison Dennis and Laura Jane (Hanks) Dennis and was married to Lela C. (Tripp) Davis.

According to his World War I Draft Registration card, he was short, slender, and had black hair and brown eyes. (www.ancestry.com)

OSCAR ALONZO DENTON, PVT., US ARMY/MARINE

Born 11-22-1895 – Died 10-6-1918 in France

He was killed in action in Fleville, France, and was buried in the Meuse-Argonne American Cemetery in Romagne, France. He was the son of Lewis Denton and Louisa (White) Denton and was married to Maud Lee (Wilson) Denton. (findagrave.com)

He was inducted at Hartville, MO on 4-26-1918 and served with the 338th Infantry to 8-16-1918 and with Co. G, 2nd Battalion, 28th Infantry Regiment, 1st Infantry Division to 10-06-1918. He served overseas from 7-21-1918 to 10-06-1918. His wife, Olive Denton, of Huggins, MO was notified of his death. (Missouri Digital Heritage)

He departed from New York on 7-21-1918 aboard the *Minnekahda*. He was a private in the 28th Infantry Regiment, 1st Division. According to his World War I Draft Registration card, he was of medium build and short and had light brown hair and dark gray eyes. (www.ancestry.com)

He was awarded the Purple Heart. (HonorStates.org)

MORGAN EDWIN DODSON

Born 8-09-1892 – Died 6-13-1943

He was buried in Pea Ridge Cemetery in Wright County, MO. (findagrave.com)

He was the son of Erastus Ewing Dodson and Lucy (Fisher) Dodson and was married to Bessie Newton. According to his World War I Draft Registration card, he was of medium build and height and had brown hair and blue eyes. (www.ancestry.com)

JAMES ALFRED DUCKWORTH, PVT., US ARMY/MARINE

Born 7-21-1891 – Died 10-18-1918

He was buried in Otter Creek Cemetery at Thornfield, Ozark County, Missouri. He was the son of William Goforth Duckworth and Eliza Jane (Ely) Duckworth. (findagrave.com)

He was inducted at Gainesville, MO on 5-28-1918 and served with the 163rd DEP BRIG to 7-10-1918 and with Co. B, 18 BN US Guards until his death. (Missouri Digital Heritage)

He died stateside of pneumonia at the Military Training Camp Hospital at Fort Brady, Michigan. His body was shipped by rail to Springfield, MO and then on to Mansfield. Family members from neighboring Ozark County met the train to carry him home for burial in the cemetery located on land donated by his parents from their homestead.

According to his World War I Draft Registration card, he was of medium build and height and had dark brown hair and blue eyes. (www.ancestry.com)

JOHN FOSTER DUDLEY, SR., U.S. MARINE CORPS

Born 11-20-1884 – Died 3-22-1937

He was buried in the Seymour Masonic Cemetery in Seymour, MO. He was the son of Stephen Foster Dudley and Sarah Elizabeth (Johnson) Dudley and was married to Sallee Rebecca (Bolender) Dudley. (findagrave.com)

According to his World War I Draft Registration card, he was of medium build and height and had brown hair and gray eyes. (www.ancestry.com)

LOUIS MARTIN EDENS, 1st LT., US ARMY/MARINE (POW)

Born 8-28-1885 – Died 2-10-1947

He was buried in Cabool Cemetery in Texas County, MO. He was the son of William Edens and Mary Augusta (Fenske) Edens. He was first married to Claire B. (Smith) Edens and later to Naoma Katherine (Leake) Edens. (findagrave.com)

He graduated from Kansas City Medical College in 1907 and came to Cabool as a young man to practice his chosen profession. During WWI he was twice wounded and was a German prisoner of war. (www.ancestry.com)

He was inducted on 7-25-1917 and served in MC as 1st LT. He served overseas from 8-29-1917 to 1-31-1919. (Missouri Digital Heritage)

GLEN HOBART EDWARDS, PVT., US ARMY/MARINE

Born 9-21-1896 – Died 10-16-1918

He was buried in Attica Cemetery in Attica, Kansas. He was the son of Daniel Zebulon

Edwards and Birtha E. (Oren) Edwards. (findagrave.com)

He was inducted at Hartville, MO on 9-03-1918 and served with Co. 4, 15th BN MED DEPT Camp Greenleaf, GA until his death from pneumonia lobar; his father, Daniel Z. Edwards of Mansfield, MO, was notified of his death. (Missouri Digital Heritage)

According to his World War I Draft Registration card, he was of medium height and build and had dark brown hair and blue eyes. (www.ancestry.com)

EDGAR LEE ELLIOTT, PVT., US ARMY

Born 3-09-1896 – Died 10-17-1918 in Alsace, France

He was buried in the Jefferson Barracks National Cemetery in Lemay Township, St. Louis, MO. He was the son of John Abraham Elliott and Susan Mary Ann (Burton) Elliott. (findagrave.com)

He was inducted at Ava, MO on 5-28-1918 and departed from New York on 8-15-1918 aboard the *Kashmir*. According to his World War I Draft Registration card, he was slender, of medium height, and had light brown hair and gray eyes. (www.ancestry.com)

He served with the 163rd DEP BRIG, Camp Dodge, IA to 5-28-1918 and with Co. G, 350th Infantry until his death. He served overseas from 8-15-1918 to 10-17-1918. He died of influenza; his mother, Mrs. Susie Elliott of Prior, MO, was notified of his death. (Missouri Digital Heritage)

He was awarded the Purple Heart and the World War I Victory Medal. (HonorStates.org)

DAVID STONE ELLIS, PVT., US ARMY

Born 2-21-1894 – Died 11-22-1955

He was buried in the Seymour Masonic Cemetery in Seymour, MO. He was the son of William Carrol Ellis and Stella Mary (Snodgrass) Ellis. He was married to Mae Tisha (Chaffin) Ellis on 12-31-1922. (findagrave.com)

He was inducted at Hartville, MO on 4-14-1918 and served with Co. B, Iowa State College TNG DET to 6-12-1918, with Field Artillery REPL DEP Camp Jackson, SC to 8-06-1918, with BTRY AUT REPL Draft, Camp Jackson, SC., with Field Artillery MTR TR CENTRE APO 994 to 12-09-1918, and with Co. B, 160th Infantry until his discharge. He was overseas from 8-22-1918 to 3-18-1919. (Missouri Digital Heritage)

He departed from Newport News, VA on 8-22-1918 aboard the *Czaritza*. He served with the 18th Battery Camp Dodge Det No. 3 of the 160th Infantry. He returned home to the U.S. on 3-6-1919 aboard the *Walter A Luckenbach* from Bordeaux, France. (www.ancestry.com)

According to his World War I Draft Registration card, he was a single, 24-year-old schoolteacher residing in Mountain Grove, MO. He was of medium height and weight, with light-colored hair and blue eyes. (www.ancestry.com)

LEE ELY, SEAMAN 1st CLASS, US NAVY

Born 8-23-1895 – Died 1-07-1980

He was buried in Little Creek Cemetery in Wright County, MO. He was the son of John Robert "Rock" Ely and Rebecca Ann (Kelley) Ely and was married to Mary Edith (Fisher) Ely. (findagrave.com)

He enlisted in the Navy on 5-08-1917. He trained at Great Lakes, IL with the Cleveland Guards; he later graduated from Quartermaster School. While he was making his sixth trip across the Atlantic, he was serving on the troop transport *U.S.S. Covington* when she was torpedoed and sank with a loss of six lives. Her ports were Hoboken, New Jersey and Brest, France. He served on the *U.S.S. Buffalo*, a repair or mother ship, keeping ships in repair. While on the *Buffalo*, he was stationed at Gibraltar, Spain for six months and Ponte Delgada Azores Islands for six months. He was awarded the Victory Medal, Service Ribbons, and 2 Gold Chevrons. He was a Seaman First Class and was discharged on 9-30-1919. (Clarence King Post American Legion's *Service Record Book*)

JOSEPH FRANKLIN EVANS, PVT., US ARMY

Born 8-13-1890 - Died 10-25-1918 in France

He died of pneumonia and was buried in the Hericourt American Cemetery in France. In May 1921 he was returned to the US on the *USAT Wheaton*. He was then buried in the Hillcrest Cemetery in Mountain Grove, MO. The inscription on his tombstone reads "88th DIV 313 AMB. TR." He was the son of Edward S. Evans and Margaret "Maggie" (Smith) Evans. He volunteered on 6-01-1918 and was stationed at Camp Dodge, IA. He served in the 350th Ambulance Co. and the 323rd Sanitary Training. (findagrave.com)

According to his World War I Draft Registration card, he was of medium height and build and had light brown hair and blue eyes. He departed from New York on 8-07-1918 aboard the *Vedic*. www.ancestry.com)

He served overseas from 8-17-1917 to 10-25-1918. His mother, Mrs. Margaret Evans of Mountain Grove, MO, was notified of his death. (Missouri Digital Heritage)

He was awarded the World War I Victory Medal. (HonorStates.org)

CLIFFORD EARL FERRELL, PVT. 1st CLASS, US ARMY/MARINE

Born 10-01-1898 – Died 4-01-1931

He was buried in the Seymour Masonic Cemetery in Seymour, MO. The inscription on his tombstone reads "Wagoner – 140th Infantry – 35th Division." He was the son of John Ferrell and Martha M. (Lipsco) Cutshall and was married to Susan Faye (Longwith) Ferrell. (findagrave.com)

He was inducted at Cabool, MO on 6-23-1917 and served as a wagoner with Co. F, 6th Infantry Missouri NG, Co. F, 140th Infantry, 35th Division to 1-14-1918, and Supply Co. 140th Infantry. (Missouri Digital Heritage)

GEORGE ELMER FINDLEY, PVT., US ARMY

Born 10-03-1890 – Died 10-05-1918 in France

He was buried in Findley Cemetery in Mansfield, MO. He was the son of George Nathaniel "Boss" Findley and Martha Evaline "Eva" (Moore) Findley. (findagrave.com)

He was inducted at Hartville, MO on 7-05-1918 and served with Co. H, 11th BN 4th REG Infantry REPL & TNG BN to 8-15-1918, with AUT REPL Draft Camp McArthur to 8-22-1918, with 364th Casual Co. to 9-22-1918, and with the 162nd Infantry, Co. B until his death. He served overseas from 8-31-1918 to 10-05-1918. He died from bronchial pneumonia; his father, George Findley of Macomb, MO, was notified of his death. (Missouri Digital Heritage)

He was awarded the World War I Victory Medal. (HonorStates.org)

JAMES HARVE FINDLEY, PVT., US ARMY/MARINE

Born 10-31-1892 – Died 2-03-1966

He was buried in Findley Cemetery in Wright County, MO. He was the son of James Henderson Findley and Severia Elizebeth Findley and was married to Ollie E. Findley. (findagrave.com)

He enlisted at Hartville, MO on 5-13-1918. He served in Co. A, 7th Armored Troop, 7th Division. He was discharged on 5-27-1919. (Clarence King Post American Legion's *Service Record Book*)

He served overseas from 8-18-1918 to 5-13-1919. (Missouri Digital Heritage)

He departed for home on 5-05-1919 from Brest, France aboard the *Von Steuben* and arrived in Hoboken, New Jersey on 5-13-1919. According to his World War I Draft Registration card, he was of medium build, tall, and had dark hair and brown eyes. (www.ancestry.com)

SAMUEL DAVID FLOYD, PVT. 1st CLASS, US ARMY/NATIONAL GUARD

Born 3-03-1892 – Died 9-28-1918 in France

He was killed in Charpentry, France and was buried in the Meuse-Argonne American Cemetery and Memorial in Lorraine, France. The inscription on his tombstone reads "PVT. 1CL. 140 INF. 35 DIV. MISSOURI." (findagrave.com)

He was the son of James N. Floyd and Julia F. Floyd. He departed from Brooklyn, NY on 4-25-1918 aboard the *Shropshire*. (www.ancestry.com)

He was inducted at Cabool, MO on 6-04-1917 and served with Co. F, 6th Infantry Missouri NG and with Co. F, 140th Infantry, 35th Division until his death. He served overseas from 4-25-1918 to 9-28-1918. He was killed in action; his father,

James Floyd of Rayborn, MO, was notified of his death. (Missouri Digital Heritage)

JOHN WILLIAM EARL FOSTER, PVT., US ARMY

Born 3-11-1896 – Died 11-11-1918 in France, before the guns went silent

He was buried at the Mount Ararat Cemetery in Douglas County, MO. The inscription on his tombstone reads "CO D 316 Inf WWI." He was the son of Robert Alexander Foster and Eary Etta Martha Lucinda Emmaline Foster and was married to Flossie Ida Ellen (Hafner) Foster. (findagrave.com)

He departed from New York on 8-24-1918 aboard the *Caronia* to serve with the Camp McArthur August Automatic Repl Draft Infantry Co. 7. According to his World War I Draft Registration card, he was tall, slender, and had dark brown hair and gray eyes. (www.ancestry.com)

He was inducted at Ava, MO on 7-5-1918 and served with Co. L, 12th BN Infantry REPL CAMP TO and Co. D, 316th Infantry until his death. He served overseas from 8-24-1918 to 11-11-1918. He was killed in action; his wife, Mrs. Flossie Foster of Prior, MO, was notified of his death. (Missouri Digital Heritage)

He was awarded the Purple Heart and the World War I Victory Medal. (HonorStates.org)

GEORGE BURNEY FREEMAN, PVT., US ARMY/MARINE

Born 8-16-1889 – Died 2-06-1960

He was the son of Marion A. Freeman and Bertie "Birdie" E. (Gorman) Freeman. According to his World War I Draft Registration card, he was slender, of medium height, and had light-colored hair and gray eyes. (www.ancestry.com)

He was inducted at St. Louis, MO on 8-03-1918 and served overseas from 9-14-1918 to 7-13-1919. (Missouri Digital Heritage)

He departed from New York on 9-14-1918 aboard the *Matsonia*. He was a private serving with Co. C, 804th Pioneer Infantry. He departed for home on 7-07-1919 from Brest, France aboard the *Imperator*. He arrived in Hoboken, New Jersey on 7-13-1919. (www.ancestry.com)

JOSEPH ALVA FREEMAN, PVT., US ARMY

Born 7-29-1891 – Died 11-05-1948

He was buried in Mound Grove Cemetery in Independence, MO. He was the son of Avery V. Freeman and Mary E. (Kittrell) Freeman and was married to Elsie Mina (Mueck) Freeman. They resided in Macomb, MO. (findagrave.com)

He served with Co. F, 354th Infantry. According to his World War I Draft Registration card, he was of medium height and build and had brown hair and blue eyes. He departed for home on 1-20-1919 from St. Nazaire, France aboard the *Mongolia*. He arrived in Hoboken, New Jersey on 1-30-1919. (www.ancestry.com)

WILLIAM EDGAR FREEMAN, PVT., US ARMY/MARINE

Born 3-11-1895 - Died 12-07-1917

He was buried in Martin Cemetery in Sycamore, MO. He was the son of John Alexander Freeman and Sina (Siney) Evaline Smith and was married to Pearl Russell. He was inducted at Gainesville, MO on 9-18-1917 and served with BTRY C, 342nd Field Artillery and BTRY D, 130th Field Artillery. He died of pneumonia; his father,

John Freeman of Zanoni, MO was notified of his death. (Missouri Digital Heritage)

He was awarded the Purple Heart. (HonorStates.org)

RAY LEOREN FRITZ, PVT., US ARMY/MARINE/NATIONAL GUARD

Born 1-11-1897 – Died 3-26-1971

He was buried in Steele Memorial Cemetery in Hartville, MO. He was the son of Roy L. Fritz and Emma Fritz and was married to Macie Lovella Fritz. (findagrave.com)

He was inducted in Hartville, MO on 9-16-1918 and served with the 57th DEP BRIG to 11-03-1918 and Co. 42, Camp McArthur, TX OCT AUT REPL DRAFT until his discharge on 12-22-1918. He also belonged to the National Guard. (Missouri Digital Heritage)

According to his World War I Draft Registration card, he was of medium height and build and had black hair and gray eyes. (www.ancestry.com)

CHARLES HOWARD FRY, PVT., US ARMY/MARINE (Older brother of Evans and Wesley Fry)

Born 12-15-1890 – Died 3-23-1947

He was buried in Fry Cemetery in Mansfield, MO. He was the son of Henry Fry and Nancy Catherine (Atkisson) Fry. (findagrave.com)

He was inducted at Hartville, MO on 7-25-1918 and served with BTRY E, 29th Field Artillery until his discharge. (Missouri Digital Heritage)

According to his World War I Draft Registration card, he was of medium height, slender, and had light-colored hair and blue eyes. (www.ancestry.com).

EVANS FRY (Younger brother of Charles Fry and older brother of Wesley Fry)

Born 12-28-1891 – Died 1-24-1975

He was buried in Hillcrest Cemetery in Mountain Grove, MO. He was the son of Henry Fry and Nancy Catherine (Atkisson) Fry and was married to Ollie E. (Key) Fry. (findagrave.com)

According to his World War I Draft Registration card, he was of medium height, slender, and had red hair and blue eyes. (www.ancestry.com)

WESLEY WOODARD FRY (Younger brother of Charles H. Fry and Evans Fry)

Born 10-31-1893 – Died 4-12-1976

He was buried in Hensley Cemetery in Wright County, MO.

He was the son of Henry Fry and Nancy Catherine (Atkisson) Fry and was married to Vergie Etta (Dennis) Fry. (findagrave.com)

According to his World War I Draft Registration card, he was tall, slender, and had brown hair and light blue eyes. (www.ancestry.com)

ALVA H. GARTIN, MECH, US ARMY

Born 7-22-1893 – Died 10-26-1918 in France

He was buried in Pleasant Hill Cemetery in Texas County, MO. He was the son of Parkison Gartin and Nancy Elizabeth (Hale) Gartin. (findagrave.com)

He was inducted at Cabool, MO on 6-04-1917 and served with Co. F, 6th Missouri Infantry, Co. F, 140th Infantry from 6-04-1917 to 10-26-1918. He served overseas from 4-25-1918 to 10-26-1918. He died from wounds received in action; his father, Parkison Gartin of Mountain Grove, MO was notified of his death. (Missouri Digital Heritage)

He was awarded the World War I Victory Medal and the Purple Heart. (HonorStates.org)

ENOCH PRESTON GASKILL (Older brother of Evan Gaskill)

Born 12-10-1877 – Died 6-16-1966

He was buried in the Nancy Newton Cemetery in Wright County, MO. He was the son of Robert Hewy Gaskill and Angeline (Newton) Gaskill. (findagrave.com)

According to his World War I Draft Registration card, he was of medium height and build and had red hair and blue eyes. (www.ancestry.com)

ERNEST ELWOOD GASKILL, PVT., US ARMY/MARINE

Born 12-10-1892 – Died 10-11-1960

He was buried at Number 5 Cemetery in Wright County, MO. He was the son of Martin Alfred Gaskill and Alice Lovenia (Ross) Gaskill. He was married to Opal Alma (Newton) Gaskill. (findagrave.com)

According to his World War I Draft Registration card, he was short, slender, had light brown hair and gray eyes, and was a farmer. He was inducted on 10-2-1917 at Hartville, MO and served with Company I, 110th Engineers. He served overseas from 5-2-1918 to 4-19-1919 and returned to the U.S. from Brest, France aboard the *Von Steuben*. (www.ancestry.com)

EVAN DEA GASKILL, MECH, US ARMY/MARINE (Younger brother of Enoch Gaskill)

Born 4-12-1893 – Died 2-11-1958

He was buried in Nancy Newton Cemetery, Wright County, MO. He was the son of Robert Hewy Gaskill and Angeline (Newton) Gaskill and was married to Clara Aslee (Marley) Gaskill. (findagrave.com)

He was inducted at Hartville and served as a mechanic with BTRY E, 29th Field Artillery. (*Missouri State Archives*)

According to his World War I Draft Registration card, he was 5'6", 150 lbs., with light complexion, gray hair, and blue eyes. (www.ancestry.com)

GEORGE WASHINGTON GASKILL, JR., PVT., US ARMY/MARINE

Born 5-27-1873 – Died 5-29-1961

He was buried in the IOOF Cemetery in Holt County, MO. The inscription on his tombstone reads "PFC CO B 38 INFANTRY WORLD WAR I." He was the son of George Washington Gaskill and Susannah Christina (Fast) Gaskill and was married to Anna Pearl (McElhaney) Gaskill. (findagrave.com)

He was inducted at Hartville, MO on 6-24-1918 and served with the 162nd DEP BRIG to 9-23-1918, with Co. 27, Camp Pike SEPT AUTO REPL Draft to 10-24-1918, with Co. M, 161st Infantry to 10-27-1918, and with Co. B, 38th Infantry until his discharge. He served overseas from 9-30-1918 to 8-20-1919. (Missouri Digital Heritage)

According to his World War I Draft Registration card, he was of medium height, stout, and had brown and red hair and brown eyes. (www.ancestry.com)

EARL RAYMOND GILLEY, SEAMAN 2ND CLASS, US NAVY

Born 1-28-1899 – Died 3-18-1974.

He was buried at Saint Joseph Memorial Park, Saint Joseph, MO. Per the 1950 Missouri Census, he was working in meat packing. (findagrave.com)

He enlisted at the Recruiting Station in Kansas City, MO on 5-27-1918. He served at the Naval Training Station in Great Lakes, IL, at the Naval Training Station in Norfolk, VA, and aboard the *USS New Mexico* from 7-19-1918 to 11-11-1918. He was discharged as a Seaman 2nd Class. (Missouri Digital Heritage)

WILLIAM RICHARD GREENWOOD, US ARMY

Born 2-7-1893 – Died 3-17-1979

He was buried in the Mansfield Cemetery. He was the son of John E. Greenwood and Lydia M. Greenwood. He was married to Cozella Eliza (Christy) Greenwood. (findagrave.com)

According to his World War I Draft Registration card, he was of medium height, stout, and had black hair and black eyes. (www.ancestry.com)

He was inducted at Indianola, IA on 7-24-1918 and served with Company A, 312th Infantry. He was overseas from 9-28-1918 to 5-25-1919. (Missouri Digital Heritage)

PAUL EDWIN GRESHAM, SEAMAN 2ND CLASS, US NAVY

Born 4-24-1897 – Died 10-05-1918

He was buried in Mount Hope Cemetery in Mound City, MO. He was the son of Nola Fee and Louisa Belle Gresham. (findagrave.com)

He was from Hartville, MO and enlisted at the Recruiting Station in St. Louis, MO on 7-10-1918. He served at the Naval Training Station in Great Lakes, IL and the Navy Rifle Range at Camp Logan, IL. He died on 10-05-1918 on the Navy Rifle Range at Camp Logan, IL. (Missouri Digital Heritage)

According to his World War I Draft Registration card, he was of medium height and build and had light brown hair and blue eyes. (www.ancestry.com)

ROY L. HANDY, WAG., US ARMY/MARINE

Born 3-7-1898 – Died 11-11-1972

He was buried at Hillcrest Cemetery, Mountain Grove, MO. He was the son of Robert L. Handy and Mamie H. Handy and was married to Elverta Catherine (Coats) Handy. (findagrave.com)

He was inducted at Mansfield, MO on 6-27-1917. He was overseas from 4-25-1918 to 4-28-1919. (Missouri Digital Heritage)

He departed from Brooklyn, New York on 4-25-1918 aboard the *Shropshire*. He departed for home from St. Nazaire, France on 4-15-1919 aboard the *Nansemond*. (www.ancestry.com)

He enlisted in the Army on 6-17-1917. He trained at Camp Clark, Missouri and Camp Doniphan, Oklahoma. He served in France as a wagoner with Supply Co., 140th Infantry, 35th Division and was discharged on 5-13-1919 at Camp Funston, Kansas. (Clarence King Post American Legion's *Service Record Book*)

ORRAN LYLE "SHORTY" HASSLER PVT., US ARMY/MARINE

Born 12-02-1897 – Died 4-18-1963

He was buried in the Chadwick Cemetery in Chadwick, MO and served with Co. 47, 12 Bn. 163rd Brig. and with Co. M., 1st Reg. Iowa Infantry Cas. Det #18, 163rd Depot Brigade. The inscription on his tombstone reads "IOWA 47 CO 163 DEPOT BRIGADE WORLD WAR I." He was the son of John Hassler and Margaret

(Alfrey) Hassler and was married to Gemonne (Loomis) Hassler. (findagrave.com)

He entered the service on April 19, 1917. He was discharged in December 1918. (Clarence King Post American Legion's *Service Record Book)*

According to his World War I Draft Registration card, he was of medium height and build and had light brown hair and blue eyes. (www.ancestry.com)

LEWIS WALTER HEATHERLY, PVT., US ARMY/MARINE

Born 7-19-1885 – Died 4-27-1918

He was buried in Turkey Creek Cemetery in Douglas County, MO. The inscription on his stone reads "26th Co. 164th D B." He was the son of William Thomas Heatherly and Herriett Jane (Hodge) Heatherly. (findagrave.com)

He was inducted at Larissa, MO on 2-25-1918 and served with the 164th DEP BRIG until his death. He died of lobar pneumonia; his father, Will Heatherly of Larissa, MO, was notified of his death. (Missouri Digital Heritage)

He was awarded the Purple Heart. (HonorStates.org)

CLARENCE EDWARD HENSLEY, ENGINEMAN 2ND CLASS, US NAVY

Born 5-13-1894 in Hartville, MO – Died 3-31-1959

He was buried at St. Matthew Cemetery in St. Louis, MO. He was the son of Charles Hensley and Janie (Campbell) Hensley and was married to Lillian V. (Tremper) Hensley and Daisy Beuanna (Adams) Owens. (findagrave.com)

He enlisted at the Recruiting Station in Salt Lake City, Utah on 8-03-1917 and served on the receiving ship at Puget Sound, WA; the receiving ship *U.S.S. Alabama* at Philadelphia, PA; the receiving ship at NY; the receiving ship at Norfolk, VA; and the *U.S.S. Lake Moor* in the Navy Yard in NY. He was discharged on 1-25-1919 as an Engineman 2nd Class. (Missouri Digital Heritage)

According to his World War I Draft Registration card, he was of medium height, slender, and had light brown hair and light brown eyes. (www.ancestry.com)

He was a freight clerk for the Wabash Railroad. (Missouri Vital Records)

ROSCOE C. HENSLEY, US ARMY/MARINE

Born 8-19-1890 – Died 2-27-1948

He was buried in Highland Cemetery in Casper, Wyoming. He was the son of John Alexander Hensley and Eliza Caroline (Smith) Hensley who were both buried in Hensley Cemetery, Mansfield, MO. (findagrave.com)

He was inducted at Hartville, MO on 7-25-1918. He served with HC Company, 41st Infantry. (Missouri Digital Heritage)

According to his World War I Draft Registration card, he was of medium height and build and had black hair and gray eyes. His occupation was listed as an oil refinery worker. (www.ancestry.com)

ROY L. HENSLEY, PVT., US ARMY/ MARINE

Born 2-23-1893 – Died 3-09-1965

He was buried in the Mansfield Cemetery in Mansfield, MO. He was the son of John Marshall Hensley and Emma (Jones) Hensley and was married to Frances A. Hensley. (findagrave.com)

He was inducted at Hartville, MO on 7-25-1918 and served with Co. F, 70th Infantry, 10th Division at Camp Funston, KS. He was discharged on 1-31-1919. (Clarence King Post American Legion's *Service Record Book)*

CARL MCKINLEY HENSON, US ARMY/MARINE

Born 11-6-1896 in OK – Died 5-6-1986 in KS

He was the son of Rev. Jonathan F. Henson and Julia F. Henson and was married to Mildred (Estsey) Henson. (findagrave.com)

He was inducted at Hartville, MO on 9-6-1918 and served with the 57th Depot Brigade. (Missouri Digital Heritage)

According to his World War I Draft Registration card, he was of medium height and build and had dark brown hair and brown eyes. (www.ancestry.com)

JOHN W. HICKS, PVT., US ARMY/ MARINE

Born 4-04-1894 – Died 10-13-1918

He was inducted at Springfield, MO on 7-14-1918 and served with Co. D, 7th BN Infantry REPL & TRN Camp McArthur, TX to 9-17-1918 and with Co. 29 SEPT AUT REPL Camp McArthur, TX until his death. He served overseas from 9-29-1918 to 10-13-1918. He died of broncho pneumonia; his sister, Mamie Denney of Seymour, MO, was notified of his death. (Missouri Digital Heritage)

CHESSLEY HIRE, PVT., US ARMY

Born 5-15-1891 – Died 2-02-1919 in France

He died in Lorraine, France and was buried in the Mansfield Cemetery in Mansfield, MO. He was the son of Cyrus and Margaret Francina Hire. (findagrave.com)

He was inducted at Hartville, MO on 5-28-1918 and served with the 163rd DEP BRIG to 6-14-1918 and with Co. F, 350th Infantry until his death. He served overseas from 8-11-1918 to 2-02-1919. He died of peritonitis; his wife, Edith Hire of Mansfield, MO, was notified of his death. (Missouri Digital Heritage)

His family requested that his remains be brought home. He was transported home from Cherbourg, France on 5-01-1921 aboard the *UST Wheaton* and arrived in Hoboken, New Jersey. According to his World War I Draft Registration card, he was of medium height and build and had black hair and brown eyes. (www.ancestry.com)

He was awarded the World War I Victory Medal. (HonorStates.org)

ORVILLE A. (HOFFORD) HOFFARTH, US ARMY/MARINE

Lest We Forget Memorial, Hartville, MO

Born 2-08-1888 – Died 1-03-1970

He was buried in Hillcrest Cemetery in Mountain Grove, MO. He was the son of Charles Henry and Mary Alice (Mitchem) Hoffarth, who lived in Wright County. He was married to Etta L. (Bartholow) Hoffarth.

According to his draft registration card, he was married, tall, of slender build, and had brown hair and brown eyes. (www.ancestry.com)

CECIL RAY HOOVER, CPL., US ARMY/MARINE

Born 4-05-1894 – Died 7-14-1933

He was the son of David William Hoover and Mary Victoria (Jenkins) Hoover. (www.ancestry.com)

He was inducted at Kansas City on 7-05-1918. He served with the 57th DEP BRIG to 9-16-1918, with Co. 15, SEPT AUT REPL DRAFT at CAMP MCARTHUR, TX to 10-29-1918, with Co. A 29 to 10-19-1918, and then with Co. A, 162nd Infantry until his discharge. He served overseas from 9-22-1918 to 2-16-1919. (Missouri Digital Heritage)

He departed on 9-21-1918 aboard the *NY#111*. He left for home on 2-08-1919 from Brest, France aboard the *Canopic*, arriving in New York on 2-19-1919. According to his World War I Draft Registration card, he was tall, slender, and had light-colored hair and blue eyes. (www.ancestry.com)

FRANK DAVE HOOVER, SGT., US ARMY/MARINE
Born 8-28-1898 – Died 1-19-1970

He was buried at Atwood Fairview Cemetery in Atwood, KS. He was the son of David W. Hoover and Mary Victoria (Jenkins) Hoover and was married to Maye (Thompson) Hoover. (findagrave.com)

He enlisted on 6-27-1917 at Mansfield, MO and departed from Brooklyn, New York on 4-25-1918 aboard the *Shropshire*. He departed for home from St. Nazaire, France on 4-15-1919 aboard the *Nansemond* and was discharged on 5-13-1919. (www.ancestry.com)

He served with Supply Co., 140th Infantry, 35th Division as a wagoner. He served overseas from 4-25-1918 to 5-13-1919. (Missouri Digital Heritage)

OTHO GEORGE HOPEWELL, APPRENTICE SEAMAN, US NAVY

Born 7-29-1896 – Died 7-25-1917

He was buried in Brushy Knob Cemetery in Douglas County, MO. He was the son of Hattie Hopewell. (findagrave.com)

He was inducted at a recruiting station in Denver, CO on 5-29-1914 and served as a Second Class Gunner's Mate. He died on 7-25-1917 at the USS A-7 Naval Hospital in Canacao, Philippines. (Missouri Digital Heritage)

He died from burns and smoke inhalation suffered the previous day in a gasoline explosion and fire aboard the USS A-7 (formerly USS Shark) submarine. (Information courtesy of David Wright)

ROY DICKERSON HUGGANS

Born 9-28-1889 – Died 1-10-1970

He was buried in Hensley Cemetery in Wright County, MO. He was the son of William Huggans and Emily S. Huggans and was married to Verba Jane "Verbie" (Spence) Huggans. According to his World War I Draft Registration card, he was tall, of medium build, and had black hair and blue eyes. (www.ancestry.com)

JOHN W. HUNT, JR., SEAMAN 2nd CLASS, U. S. NAVY

Born 11-06-1889 - Died 10-17-1917 in France

He was a member of the SS Antilles Unit. He was listed as missing in action or lost at sea. He received the Purple Heart. (HonorStates.org)

He was buried or memorialized in the Tablets of the Missing section of the Suresnes American Cemetery in Paris, France.

According to his draft registration card, he was married, short, of medium build, and had light brown hair and light blue eyes. (www.ancestry.com)

ZECK (ZEEK) HURST, PVT., US ARMY

Born 9-04-1886 – Died 10-18-1918

He was buried in Hurst Cemetery in Douglas County, MO. He was the son of Samuel Hurst, Jr. and Sarah (Anthy) Hurst. (findagrave.com)

He was inducted at Ava, MO on 5-28-1918 and served with Co. E, 350th Infantry until his death. He served overseas from 8-11-1918 to 10-18-1918. He died from influenza; his father, Samuel Hurst of Bertha, MO, was notified of his death. (Missouri Digital Heritage)

He was awarded a World War I Victory Medal. (HonorStates.org)

THOMAS CORVAN INGRAHAM, SGT., US ARMY

Born 11-2-1892 – Died 9-5-1918 in France

He was buried in Hillcrest Cemetery in Mountain Grove, MO. He was the son of Thomas Corwin and Mary Francis Ingraham. (findagrave.com)

He was inducted in Augusta, KS on 7-16-1917 and served with Co. F, 3rd Infantry Kansas NG and with Co. F, 139th Infantry until his death. He served overseas from 4-25-1918 to 9-05-1918. He was accidentally killed by a rifle bullet; his mother, Mary Ingraham of Mountain Grove, MO was notified of his death. (Missouri Digital Heritage)

He departed from New York on 4-25-1918 aboard the *Caronia*. According to his World War I Draft Registration card, he was tall, stout, and had brown hair and blue eyes. (www.ancestry.com)

He was awarded the World War I Victory Medal. (HonorStates.org)

WALTER HENRY IPOCK, CPL., US ARMY/MARINE

Born 4-5-1894 – Died 12-21-1985

He was buried at Nancy Newton Cemetery, Mansfield, MO. He was the son of Zachariah Hancock Ipock and Samantha Caroline (Dudley) Ipock. He was married to Elva Marie (Goss) Ipock. (findagrave.com)

According to his World War I Draft Registration card, he was born on 4-5-1894, was single and resided in Wright County, MO. He was of medium height, medium build, and had dark brown hair and gray eyes. (www.ancestry.com)

He was inducted at Hartville, MO on 7-25-1918 and served with Battery E, 29th Field Artillery until his discharge. (Missouri Digital Heritage)

CHARLES W. JAMES, PVT. 1ST CLASS, US ARMY/MARINE

Born 12-27-1894 – Died 1-29-1959

He was the son of John W. James and Sarah James. He served with Co. B, 346th MG BN, 91st

DIV. He lived in Mansfield, MO. He departed from New York on 7-07-1918 aboard the *Darro*. He departed for home on 4-02-1919 from St. Nazaire, France aboard the *Floridian* and arrived in Hoboken, New Jersey on 4-14-1919. He served with Co. B, 346th MG BN, 91st DIV. (www.ancestry.com)

SHERMAN E. JENNINGS, PVT., US ARMY/MARINE

Born Sep 1893 – Died 12-24-1917

He was buried at Walnut Grove Cemetery in Douglas County, MO. He was the son of Jason Washington Jennings and Josephine I. (Reynolds) Jennings. He served in the 342nd Field Artillery, 89th Division. (findagrave.com) He was inducted at Ava, MO on 9-18-1917 and served with BTRY C, 342nd Field Artillery. He died at Camp Funston, KS from an attack of measles and pneumonia on 12-24-1917. J. W. Jennings of Ava, Mo was notified of his death. (Missouri Digital Heritage)

He was awarded the Purple Heart. (HonorStates.org)

LOUIS WINT JOHNSON, CPL., US ARMY

Born 11-19-1896 – Died 6-03-1918

He was buried at the Aisne-Marne American Cemetery and Memorial in Belleau, France. (findagrave.com)

According to his World War I Draft Registration card, he was of medium height and build and had light brown hair and blue eyes. He lived in Mountain Grove, MO. (www.ancestry.com)

He served overseas from 11-4-17 to 6-03-1918. He was killed in action and was awarded the Purple Heart and the World War One Victory Medal. (HonorStates.org)

IRA RUTHERFORD KEELING, PVT., US ARMY/MARINE

Born 7-1-1892 – Died 3-7-1981

He was buried at Hensley Cemetery, Wright County, MO. He was the son of Abraham Frank Keeling and Sarah Angeline (Gibson) Keeling and was married to Clema "Clemie" (Buhler) Keeling. (findagrave.com)

According to his World War I Draft Registration card, he was 5'4", 140 lbs., and had gray hair and blue eyes with a dark complexion. (www.ancestry.com)

He was inducted at Hartville on 10-2-1917 and served with the 164th Dep Brig to 10-23-1917 and with Supply Co., 129 Field Artillery until his discharge. (Missouri Digital Heritage)

THOMAS LOVELL KEELING, US ARMY/MARINE

Born 5-12-1892 – Died 9-12-1978

He was buried in the Mansfield Cemetery. He was the son of Thomas Jefferson Keeling and Mollie L. (Ivey) Keeling.(findagrave.com)

He was inducted at Hartville, MO on 10-2-1917. He served as a wagoner with the Supply Company, 129th Field Artillery and was overseas from 6-28-1918 to 3-1-1919. (Missouri Digital Heritage)

He departed from New York City on 6-28-1918 aboard the *Virginian*. According to his World War I Draft Registration card, he was tall, of medium build, and had light-colored hair and blue eyes. (www.ancestry.com)

BERTIE KELLOGG, PVT., US ARMY/MARINE

Born 12-30-1890 – Died 10-07-1918

He was inducted at Marshfield, MO on 7-14-1918 and served with Co. E, 8th BN Infantry REPL & TNG Camp to 9-17-1918 and with Co. 30 Camp McArthur Sept. AUT REPL DRAFT until his death. He served overseas from 9-29-1918 to 10-07-1918. He died of lobar pneumonia on 10-07-1918; his uncle, Clinton Kellogg of Seymour, MO, was notified of his death. (Missouri Digital Heritage)

WILLIAM ELMER KESTER, PVT., US ARMY

Born 8-29-1890 in Douglas County, MO – Died 10-27-1918 in France

He died in combat at Belleau Wood, France and was buried in the Aisne-Marne American Cemetery in Belleau, Lorraine, France. He was the son of Jeremiah M. Kester and Margaret Mahulda (Baxter) Kester.

He served in the 163rd DEP BRIG to 6-14-1918, then with Battery D. 339th FA to death. He died of broncho pneumonia. His brother-in-law of Smallet, MO was notified of his death. (Missouri Digital Heritage)

He was awarded the World War I Victory Medal. (HonorStates.org)

CLARENCE KING, PVT., US ARMY (Younger brother of Elbert King)

Born 2-7-1900 – Died 10-16-1918 in France

He was buried in the Mansfield Cemetery in Mansfield, MO.

He was the son of William King and Mary Jane King. (findagrave.com)

He departed on 4-25-1918 from New York, NY aboard the *Aeneas*. (www.ancestry.com)

He was inducted into the Army N. G. on 7-26-1917 at Seymour, MO and served with HQ Co., 6th Infantry Missouri NG HQ Co., 140th Infantry to 4-17-1918 and with Co. I, 140th Infantry, 35th Division. He served overseas from 4-25-1918 to 10-16-1918. He died on 10-16-1918 of wounds received in action in France; his mother, Mary Jane King of Mansfield, MO, was notified of his death. (Missouri Digital Heritage)

He was awarded the Purple Heart and the World War I Victory Medal. (HonorStates.org)

ELBERT H. KING, COOK, US ARMY (Older brother of Clarence King)

Born 6-26-1898 – Died 1-27-1976

He was buried in the Floral Haven Cemetery in Tulsa, Oklahoma. (www.ancestry.com)

He was the son of William King and Mary Jane (Hight) King. (findagrave.com)

He enlisted on 5-9-1917 and served as a cook. He departed from Hoboken, New Jersey on 3-14-1918 aboard the ship *85*. He served in the 119th FA as a cook. He was 6'1", weighed 225 lbs., and had a ruddy complexion, brown hair, and blue eyes. He was discharged on 5-19-1919. The 1940 census shows his occupation as Deputy Sheriff in Tulsa, OK. (www.ancestry.com)

Elbert H. King was fighting a short distance from Clarence when someone came down the road and told him that his younger brother had been killed.

(Written information taken from the back of Elbert's photo)

WILLIE LEROY, PVT., US ARMY/MARINE

Born 12-08-1893 – Died 10-14-1918

He was buried in Yates Cemetery in Douglas County, MO. He was the son of Peter "Peat" Leroy and Mary L. (Matlock) Leroy.

He was inducted at Ava, MO on 5-28-1918 and served with the 163rd DEP BRIG from 5-28-1918 to 6-14-1918 and with Co. G, 350th Infantry, 86th Division. He served overseas from 8-15-1918 to 10-14-1918. He died on 10-14-1918 from wounds received in action; his father, Pete Leroy of Bertha, MO, was notified of his death. (Missouri Digital Heritage)
He was awarded the Purple Heart. (HonorStates.org)

YAROSLOV LISKA, PVT., US ARMY/MARINE

Born 8-24-1895 – Died 10-13-1918

He was buried in Lone Star Cemetery in Mountain Grove, MO. He was the son of Bohumil (John) and Anna Liska. His father immigrated to the United States from the Czech Republic, then known as Bohemia. (findagrave.com)

He was inducted at Ava on 8-30-1918 and died at Camp Dodge, Iowa on October 13, 1918. (Missouri Digital Heritage)

According to his World War I Draft Registration card, he was of medium height and build and had brown hair and blue eyes. (www.ancestry.com)

SHELTON C. LUTTRELL, MECH., US ARMY

Born 6-25-1897 – Died 7-30-1918 in France

He was originally buried in the Argonne American Cemetery in France, but on 8-15-21, he was laid to rest in Arlington National Cemetery in VA. He was the son of John Henry Luttrell and Allie (Fleming) Luttrell.

He left from Hoboken, New Jersey on 5-22-1918 aboard the *Great Northern* to serve as a wagoner with Sup. Co. 13th FA, 4th Division. (www.ancestry.com)

He died of wounds received in action. He was awarded the Purple Heart and the World War I Victory Medal. (HonorStates.org)

JOSEPH DAVIS MASHBURN, PVT., US MARINE CORPS

Born 2-8-1898 – Died 9-1-1973

He was buried in Springfield National Cemetery, Springfield, MO. He was married to Jewell (Shumate) Mashburn. Per the 1950 Missouri Census he was working as a building contractor/carpenter in Springfield, MO. (findagrave.com)

He was inducted on 8-7-1918 at St. Louis, MO. His residence was listed as Seymour, MO. He served overseas from 11-5-1918 to 5-5-1919. He served in the 7th Separate Battalion and the 78th Co. 6th Regiment. (Missouri Digital Heritage)

CARL WILLIAM MAYS, PVT., US ARMY/MARINE (Older brother of Frank Mays)

Born 11-12-1891 – Died 4-4-1971

He was buried in Riverview Cemetery, Multnomah County, OR. He was the son of William Henry Mays and Louisa Caroline (Land) Mays. (findagrave.com)

He was inducted at Ava, MO on 11-6-1918. He served at Washington University TNG Det, St. Louis, MO until his discharge. (Missouri Digital Heritage)

His unit was the last drafted from Douglas County as the next group was turned away at Mansfield, the designated place of embarkment, since peace had been signed. He continued his Major League Baseball career the following spring. (www.ancestry.com)

FRANKLIN CRENSHAW MAYS, CPL., US ARMY/ MARINE (Younger brother of Carl Willliam Mays)

Born 3-13-1895 – Died 2-13-1976

He was buried in Prairie Hollow Cemetery in Douglas County, MO. He was the son of William Henry and Louisa Caroline (Land) Mays and was married to Ruby M. (Banfield) Mays and later to Mabel (Thompson) Mays. (findagrave.com)

He served with BTRY C 342 FA to 10-05-1917 and with HQ TR 89th DIV until discharge. He served overseas from 6-30-1918 to 10-29-1918. He departed for home to New York on 10-18-1918 aboard the *Scotian*. He was honorably discharged with 25 percent disability. (Missouri Digital Heritage)

According to his World War I Draft Registration card, he was tall and of medium build. He had light-colored hair and blue eyes. (www.ancestry.com)

OLIVER HARVEY MCMURTREY, PVT., US ARMY/MARINE

Born 12-17-1892 – Died 10-4-1918

He was buried in Hillcrest Cemetery in Mountain Grove, MO.

He was inducted at Hartville, MO on 7-25-1918 and served with Co. F, 70th Infantry. He died of lobar pneumonia on 10-04-1918; his father, David McMurtrey of Mountain Grove, MO, was notified of his death. (Missouri Digital Heritage)

According to his World War I Draft Registration card, he was tall, slender, and had dark brown hair and blue eyes. (www.ancestry.com)

VIRGIL MONROE MCMURTREY, PVT., US ARMY/MARINE

Born 10-11-1891 – Died 10-08-1918

He was buried at Sweeton Pond Cemetery in Ozark County, MO. He was the son of Daniel Orson McMurtrey and Harriet Matilda "Hattie" (Hughes) McMurtrey. (findagrave.com)

He was inducted at Ava, MO on 7-25-1918 and served with Co. A, 70th Infantry. He died of lobar pneumonia on 10-08-1918; his father, Daniel McMurtrey of Dora, MO, was notified of his death. (Missouri Digital Heritage)
He was awarded the Purple Heart. (HonorStates.org)

ARCHIE JAMES MILLER, PVT., US ARMY (Older brother of Raymond Miller)

Born 11-6-1892 – Died 7-31-1975

He was buried in Roseburg National Cemetery in Douglas County, OR. He was the son of James Oliphant Miller and Mary Leander (Findley)

Miller and was married to Jewel Lillian (Sharp) Miller. (findagrave.com)

He departed for home from Brest, France on 5-15-1919 aboard the *Leviathan*. He arrived at Hoboken, New Jersey on 5-22-1919. He served with Headquarters Co. 353rd Infantry. According to his World War I Draft Registration card, he was of medium height and build and had light-colored hair and blue eyes. (www.ancestry.com)

RAYMOND KELTON MILLER, US ARMY
(Younger brother of Archie Miller)

Born 5-31-1895 – Died 1-5-1984

He was buried in Rose Hills Memorial Park in Los Angeles County, CA. He was the son of James Oliphant Miller and Mary Leander (Findley) Miller. He was married to Ione Bethel (Lewis) Miller. (findagrave.com)

He enlisted on 10-2-1917 and was discharged on 4-29-1919.

According to his World War I Draft Registration card, he was short, of medium build, and had light-colored hair and blue eyes. (www.ancestry.com)

HARRY LESTER MOODY, CPL., US ARMY

Born 3-25-1896 – Died 2-13-1970

He was buried in Steele Memorial Cemetery in Hartville, MO. He was the son of Levi Moody and Janie (Davis) Moody and married Vada Aleth (Rippee) Moody. (www.ancestry.com)

He enlisted at Hartville, MO on 7-21-1917 and served with Co. F, 140th Infantry, 35th Division. He departed from Brooklyn, New York on 4-25-1918 aboard the *Shropshire*. He departed for home on 4-15-1919 from St. Nazaire, France aboard the *Nansemond*. According to his World War I Draft Registration card, he was of medium build and height and had brown hair and gray eyes. (www.ancestry.com)

JOHN AUSTIN MOORE, PVT., US ARMY/MARINE

Born 4-21-1895 – Died 9-11-1918 in France

He was buried in the Union Grove Cemetery in Douglas County, MO. He was the son of William Henry Moore and Katherine Barzilla (Lay) Moore. He was married to Ureth Orella (Turner) Baxter. He was inducted at Ava, MO on 4-01-1918. He served with Co. 20, 164th DEP BRIG to 4-24-1918 and with Co. H, 354th Infantry until his death. He served overseas from 6-05-1918 to 9-11-1918. He died of wounds received in action; his wife, Mrs. John A. Moore of Rome, MO, was notified of his death. (Missouri Digital Heritage)

He was awarded the Purple Heart and the World War I Victory Medal. (HonorStates.org)

JAMES ANDREW MORRIS, PVT., US ARMY/MARINE

Born 10-29-1886 – Died 10-21-1965

He was buried in the Mansfield Cemetery. He was the son of John Frederick Morris and Martha Ann (Rush) Morris and was married to Cora May (Kittrell) Morris. (findagrave.com)

He was inducted at Hartville on 5-13-1918 at 31½ years of age and served with Company M, 12th Infantry to 8-10-1918 and with Co. F, 31st Infantry to discharge. He served in Siberia from 9-2-1918 to 8-22-1919 and was discharged having a 25% disability. (Missouri Digital Heritage)

He departed on 9-2-1918 from San Francisco, CA aboard the *Logan*. He was with the Siberian Replacement Troops Camp Fremont. (www.ancestry.com)

EFTON NEWTON, US ARMY/MARINE

Born 10-1-1895 – Died 4-26-1988

He was buried in Pleasant Hill Cemetery at Hartville, MO. He was the son of William Carr Newton and Mary Etta (Pearman) Newton and was married to Velma Gladys (Fuge) Newton. (findagrave.com)

He was inducted at Hartville, MO on 10-02-1917 and served in HQ Co. FA, then BTRY B, 129th FA, and then Supply Co. 129th FA. He served overseas from 5-20-1918 to 04-20-1919. (Missouri Digital Heritage)

EZRA TRIMBLE NEWTON, PVT., US ARMY/MARINE

Born 3-9-1892 – Died 9-10-1973

He was buried in New Ross Cemetery, New Ross, Indiana. He was married to Winnie "Mae" (Johnson) Newton. (findagrave.com)

He was inducted in Douglas County, MO on 8-15-1918 and served in the 314th REP Unit MTC and then in M REP Unit 310th MTC. He served overseas from 10-28-1918 to 7-2-1919. (Missouri Digital Heritage)

HOSEA EARL NEWTON, US ARMY/MARINE (Younger brother of Ira Jason Newton)

Born 1-04-1895 – Died 9-01-1950

He was buried in Greenhill Cemetery in Rock Port, MO. He was the son of John Newton and Orlena Mahaley Newton and was married to Mary Ola (Dodson) Newton. (findagrave.com)

According to his World War I Draft Registration card, he was of medium height and build and had dark brown hair and blue eyes. (www.ancestry.com)

IRA "JASON" NEWTON, US ARMY/MARINE (Older brother of Hosea Earl Newton)

Born 8-06-1891 – Died 6-24-1969

He was buried in Hensley Cemetery in Mansfield, MO. He was the son of John Newton and Orlena Mahaley (Farrell) Newton and was married to Flora L. (Estus) Newton. (findagrave.com)

According to his World War I Draft Registration card, he was slender, of medium height, and had dark brown hair and brown eyes. (www.ancestry.com)

JESSE ALBERT NEWTON, US ARMY/ MARINE

Born 5-14-1880 – Died 4-01-1940

He was buried at Hazelwood Cemetery in Greene County, MO. He was the son of John Newton and Margaret Louisa "Eliza" (Pool) Newton and was married to Bessie Josephine (Letsinger) Allison. (findagrave.com)

JOHN ALLISON "AL" NEWTON, PVT., US ARMY (Younger brother of Mose Newton and older brother of Walter Newton)

Born 3-15-1896 – Died 5-10-1980

He was buried at Steele Memorial Cemetery in Hartville, MO. He was the son of William Jefferson Newton and Louisa Ann (Rippee) Newton and was married to Ila Mary (Buck) Newton. (findagrave.com)

He was inducted at Hartville on 5-28-1918 and served overseas as a machine gunner with Co. D, 339th MG BN from 8-16-1918 to 5-29-1919. (Missouri Digital Heritage)

He departed on 8-14-1918 from Philadelphia, Pennsylvania aboard the *Rhesus*. He departed for home from St. Nazaire, France on 5-20-1919 aboard the *USS Pastores*. According to his World War I Draft Registration card, he was tall and slender and had brown hair and blue eyes. (www.ancestry.com)

SAMMA "SAM" ELMER NEWTON, CPL., US ARMY/MARINE

Born 11-21-1889 – Died 2-15-1980.

He was buried in the Nancy Newton Cemetery in Wright County, MO. He was the son of John Marion Preston Newton and Louisa A. (Rippee) Newton and was married to Mary Jane "Jannie" White and later to Lena Pearl (Marley) Newton. (findagrave.com)

He was discharged on 2-04-1919. According to his World War I Draft Registration card, he was of medium height and build and had dark brown hair and blue eyes. (www.ancestry.com)

He was the postmaster at Cedar Gap, MO, from 1925-1935. (www.ancestry.com)

WALTER DEWEY NEWTON (Younger brother of Mose Newton and John Allison Newton)

Born 5-13-1899 in Wright County, MO – Died 10-15-1979 in Mason, IA

He was buried in Memorial Park Cemetery in Mason City, IA. He was the son of Willliam Jefferson Newton and Louisa Ann (Rippee) Newton and was married to Adelaide Versaille Newton. (findagrave.com)

According to his World War I Draft Registration card, he was tall, slender, and had dark hair and blue eyes. (www.ancestry.com)

WILLIAM MOSES "MOSE" NEWTON, PVT., US ARMY/MARINE (Older brother of John Allison Newton and Walter Dewey Newton)

Born 9-8-1893 – Died 7-11-1969

He was buried in the Nancy Newton Cemetery in Wright County, MO. The inscription on the tombstone reads "PVT CO A 70 INFANTRY WORLD WAR I." He was the son of William Jefferson Newton and Louisa Ann (Rippee) Newton and was married to Ada Mae (Rosevear) Newton. (findagrave.com)

He was inducted at Hartville on 7-25-1918 and served with Co. A, 70th Infantry. (Missouri Digital Heritage)

He was discharged on 2-04-1919. According to his World War I Draft Registration card, he was single, short, slender and had light brown hair and blue eyes. (www.ancestry.com)

ROY G. NORCROSS, SADDLER, US ARMY/MARINE

Born: 11-16-1897 - Died: 12-7-1922

He was buried in the Mansfield Cemetery. He was the son of George Henry Norcross and Molly A. Norcross. (findagrave.com)

He was inducted at Mansfield, MO on 6-27-1917 at 19 years of age. He was a saddler with Supply Co., 6th Infantry, Missouri NG and Supply Co., 140th Infantry. He was discharged with a reported 25% disability. (Missouri Digital Heritage)

According to his World War I Draft Registration card, he was of medium height and build and had light brown hair and blue eyes. (www.ancestry.com)

ERNEST A. PACKARD, WAG., US ARMY/MARINE

He was born in Peoria, KS and was inducted in Seymour, MO on 6-27-1917 and served with Supply Co., 6th Infantry Missouri NG and with Supply Co., 140th Infantry as a wagoner. He served overseas from 4-25-1918 to 4-28-1919. (Missouri Digital Heritage)

FRANK LEROY PEACOCK, Sr., US ARMY/MARINE

Born 5-25-1889 – Died 7-08-1961

He was buried in the Mansfield Cemetery in Mansfield, MO. He was the son of Franklin Leroy Peacock, Sr. and Mary Ellen (Bratcher) Peacock and was married to Verba M. (Turner) Peacock. (findagrave.com)

According to his World War I Draft Registration card, he was married, tall, of stout build, and had light hair and blue eyes. (www.ancestry.com)

BURL PHILLIPS, PVT., US ARMY

Born 7-16-1893 – Died 10-02-1918 in France

He was buried in the Meuse-Argonne American Cemetery and Memorial in Romagne, France. The inscription on his tombstone reads "PVT. 139 INF. 35 DIV." He was the son of Jesse A. Phillips and Nancy "Nannie" (Thomas) Phillips. (findagrave.com)

He was inducted in Ava, MO on 9-18-1917. He served with BTRY C, 342nd Field Artillery to 10-15-1917, with Co. 22, 16th DEP BRIG to Oct. 1917, with M Co. 3, 110th AM TN to 12-16-1917, and with Co. H, 139th Infantry, until his death. He served overseas from 4-25-1918 to 10-02-1918. He died of wounds received in action; his father, Jesse Phillips of Roy, MO was notified of his death. (Missouri Digital Heritage)

He was awarded the Purple Heart and the World War I Victory Medal. (HonorStates.org)

CLARENCE PLASTER, PVT., US ARMY/MARINE

Born 1-05-1896 – Died 8-13-1921

He was buried in Souder Cemetery in Ozark County, MO. He was the son of Samuel P. and Sarah L. Plaster. (findagrave.com)

He was inducted at Marshfield, MO on 5-28-1918 and served overseas from 8-11-1918 to 5-30-1919. (Missouri Digital Heritage)

He departed from Brooklyn, New York on 8-11-1918 on the *Delta*. He was a member of Company F, 350th Infantry. According to his World War I Draft Registration card, he was single, tall, slender, and had light brown hair and brown eyes. (www.ancestry.com)

CARLYLE POE, BN. SGT. MAJ., US ARMY

Born 7-11-1889 – Died 11-27-1958

He was buried at Hillcrest Cemetery in Mountain Grove, MO. The inscription on his tombstone reads "BN SGT MAJ HQ DEPT 89 DIV WORLD WAR I." findagrave.com)

He was the son of James E. Poe and Gillie Poe and was married to Eunice (Bowlin) Poe. (www.ancestry.com)

He enlisted at Hartville, MO on 10-02-1917 and served with the HQ DET, 89th DIV. at Camp Funston, KS, with HQ Co., 356th Infantry, and then HQ DET, 89th DIV. at Camp Funston, until his discharge on 6-13-1919. He was overseas from 6-03-1918 to 5-31-1919. (Missouri Digital Heritage)

He departed from New York on 6-04-1918 aboard the *Caronia*. He departed for home on 5-20-1919 from Brest, France aboard the *Rotterdam*. According to his World War I Draft Registration card, he was of medium height and build and had brown hair and blue eyes. (www.ancestry.com)

FRANK POPE, SGT., ARMY/MARINE

Born 3-27-1885 - Died 6-09-1954

He was buried in Bowers Chapel Cemetery in Urbana, MO. He was the son of Nathan Kinzie Pope, Sr. and Mary Jane (Creed) Pope and was married to Lula (Manning) Pope. He was inducted at Hartville, MO on 10-03-1917. He served with the 164th DEP BRIG to 8-18-1918 and with HQ DET 30 MG BN until his discharge. (Missouri Digital Heritage)

According to his World War I Draft Registration card, he was short, stout, and had black hair and dark brown eyes. (www.ancestry.com)

JOHN JASPER POTTS, WAG., US ARMY/ NATIONAL GUARD

Born 10-12-1898 – Died 12-09-1987

He was the son of Alonzo Franklin Potts and Flora Caroline Potts. (findagrave.com)

He was inducted at Mansfield, MO on 6-27-1917 at the age of 18 2/3 years. He served with the Supply Co. 6, 140th Infantry Missouri NG and with the Supply Co., 140th Infantry, 35th Division as a wagoner. He served overseas from 4-25-1918 to 4-28-1919. (Missouri Digital Heritage)

He departed from Brooklyn, New York on 4-25-1918 aboard the *Shropshire*. He departed for home from St. Nazaire, France on 4-15-1919 aboard the *Nansemond*. (www.ancestry.com)

RAYMOND ROY RILEY, US ARMY/ MARINE

Born 10-3-1893 – Died 2-3-1959

He was buried in the Mansfield Cemetery. He was the son of John J. Riley and Margaret (Hopper) Riley and was married to Opal Riley. (findagrave.com)

He served with 57 DEP BRIG to 11-23-18 and Co. G, 329th Infantry until discharge.

According to his World War I Draft Registration card, he was married, short, of slender build, and had auburn hair and blue eyes. (www.ancestry.com)

FOSTER ASBERRY RIPPEE, US ARMY/ MARINE (Older brother of Ira and Hosea Rippee)

Born 8-18-1882 – Died 6-26-1961

He was buried in the Mansfield Cemetery in Mansfield, MO. He was the son of John Rippee and Louisa "Anice" (Newton) Rippee and was married to Ida Ermintrude Oliver and then to Edna Plaster (Branstetter) Rippee. (findagrave.com)

According to his World War I Draft Registration card, he was medium height, stout, and had brown hair and blue eyes. (www.ancestry.com)

HOSEA NICHOLS RIPPEE, US ARMY/ MARINE (Younger brother of Foster Rippee and Ira Rippee)

Born 8-08-1884 – Died 4-27-1950

He died from the flu and cardiac arrest and was buried in the Mansfield Cemetery in Mansfield, MO. He was the son of John Rippee and Louisa "Anice" (Newton) Rippee. (findagrave.com)

According to his World War I Draft Registration card, he was tall, stout, and had black hair and blue eyes. (www.ancestry.com)

IRA ELI RIPPEE, PVT., US ARMY/ MARINE (Younger brother of Foster Rippee and Hosea Rippee)

Born 4-28-1888 – Died 8-01-1972

He was buried in the Mansfield Cemetery in Mansfield, MO. He was the son of John Rippee and Louisa "Anice" (Newton) Rippee. (findagrave.com)

He was inducted at Hartville on 7-25-1918 and served with BTRY F, 28th Field Artillery. (Missouri Digital Heritage)

According to his World War I Draft Registration card, he was of medium height and build and had black hair and gray eyes. (www.ancestry.com)

VERNER RIPPEE, WAG., US ARMY/ MARINE

Born 8-20-1889 – Died 12-30-1958

He was buried in the Mansfield Cemetery. He was the son of Dora Winningham and was married to Pearl Euma (Newton) Rippee. (findagrave.com)

He enlisted at Hartville on 5-28-1918 at 28 years of age and served as a wagoner with Supply Co., 350th Infantry, 88th Division. (Missouri Digital Heritage)

According to his World War I Draft Registration card, he was tall, slender, and had black hair and black eyes.

He departed on 8-11-1918 from Brooklyn, New York aboard the *Delta*. He departed for home from St. Nazaire, France on 4-19-1919 aboard the *Aeolus*. (www.ancestry.com)

CLIFTON HARVEY ROBINETT, MAJOR, US ARMY (Older brother of Paul McDonald Robinett)

Born 11-22-1890 – Died 4-28-1975

He was buried at Hillcrest Cemetery in Mountain Grove, MO. The inscription on his tombstone reads "Maj. WWI & WW2, SCW, SAR, SW 1812." He was the son of James Harvey Robinett, Jr. and Sarah Naomi (Lee) Robinett. (findagrave.com)

(S.A.R. stands for Search and Rescue)

PAUL MCDONALD ROBINETT, BRIGADIER GENERAL, US ARMY REGISTER (Younger brother of Major Clifton Robinett)

Born 12-19-1893 – Died 2-05-1975

He was buried at Hillcrest Cemetery in Mountain Grove, MO. The inscription on his tombstone reads "BRIG. GEN. PAUL M. ROBINETT, USA, SERVED IN W.W.I. AND IN NORTH AFRICA, W.W.II, VICTOR AT KASSERINE PASS, S.C.W., S.A.R., S.W. 1812." He was the son of James Harvey Robinett, Jr. and Sarah Naomi (Lee) Robinett. (findagrave.com)

He departed from Cherbourg, France aboard the *George Washington* and arrived in New York on 8-31-1924. According to his World War I Draft Registration card, he was slender, short, and had black hair and blue eyes. (www.ancestry.com)

WILLIAM JONAS "JOE" ROE, WAG., US ARMY/MARINE

Born 10-25-1884 – Died 11-22-1960

He was buried in the Springfield National Cemetery, in Greene County, MO. He was the son of Henry Roe and Martha Jane (Cline) Roe and was married to Clara Annabel (Taylor) Roe. (findagrave.com)

He was inducted in Ava, MO on 6-27-1917 and served with Supply Co., 6th Infantry Missouri NG and Supply Co., 140th Infantry as a wagoner. He served overseas from 4-25-1918 to 4-28-1919. (Missouri Digital Heritage)

DR. ROBERT M. ROGERS, VET MED SERVICE CORP.

Born Dec. 1862 – Died 6-02-1927

According to the 1900 census, he was born in Henderson, MO in Webster County and married Cara Belle "Carrie" Haskins on 11-12-1884.

He hung out his medical shingle in Mansfield in 1891. (*Mansfield Mirror* 11-8-1917)

He and his wife, Carrie, had two children: son R. B. (Russel) and daughter Agnes, who later married E. A. Sisk. (www.ancestry.com)

He stitched cuts, set bones, delivered babies, and even performed amputations when needed. (*Mansfield Mirror*)

Dr. Rogers conducted local exams of the Supply Co., 6th Regiment. (*Mansfield Mirror* 7-5-1917)

He joined the Army Medical Service with the rank of lieutenant. (*Mansfield Mirror* 7-26-1917)

He also served as Chairman of the Mansfield Red Cross Chapter and as Chairman of the Council of Medical Defense in both Wright and Douglas counties. Following the end of the war, he conducted pension examinations. *(Mansfield Mirror 8-12-1920)*

Dr. Rogers was active in Mansfield Camp No. 3448 of the Modern Woodsman where he served as Camp Physician. He also served as Chaplain of the Mansfield Masonic Lodge No. 513 AF & AM. and was trustee of the Methodist Church. *(Mansfield Mirror)*

JESSE B. ROOTE, JR., MAJOR, US ARMY/MARINE

Born 6-03-1895 - Died 11-09-1987

He departed from Hoboken, New Jersey on 12-15-1917 aboard the *Leviathan* and served with Field and Staff, 163rd Infantry. He departed for home on 9-10-1919 from Brest, France aboard the *Mount Vernon* and arrived in Hoboken, New Jersey on 9-18-1919. He served with Co. #1, US MIL MISS, BERLIN. According to his World War I Draft Registration card, he was slender, short, and had light brown hair and brown eyes. (www.ancestry.com)

ARTHUR WILLIAM ROPER, PVT., US ARMY/MARINE

Born 6-17-1896 – Died 7-10-1960

He was buried in Golden Gate National Cemetery in San Bruno, CA. (findagrave.com)

He was inducted at Ava, MO on 2-25-1918 and served with the 164th DEP BRIG to 3-28-1918 and with PFC Battery E, 340th Field Artillery, 39th Division to his discharge. He was overseas from 6-13-1918 to 5-24-1919. (Missouri Digital Heritage)

CHARLES SYLVESTER ROSS, PVT. 1st CLASS, US ARMY

Born 5-27-1899 in Dora, MO – Died 7-28-1977

He was buried in Howell Memorial Park Cemetery in Howell County, MO. The inscription on his tombstone reads "PFC US ARMY WORLD WAR I." He was married to Phoebe Ellen (Collins) Ross.

He enlisted on 7-04-1917 and was discharged on 9-16-1919. (www.ancestry.com)

He was inducted at West Plains, MO. He served with Co. D, 2nd Infantry Missouri NG, with Co. D, 128th M G BN to 3-01-1918, Co. D, 130th M G BN to 5-26-1919, and with Co. 282 M P C. He served overseas from 5-03-1918 to 9-09-1919. He was severely injured on 9-29-1918. (Missouri Digital Heritage)

ROY CALVIN RUMPLE, PVT., US ARMY

Born 4-27-1896 – Died 12-17-1975

He was buried in White Rose Cemetery in Bartlesville, OK and was married to Sarah E. Rumple and later to Lillian D. (Blackmer) Rumple. (findagrave.com)

He resided in Cedar Gap and was inducted at Sidney, IA on 7-22-1918 and served with 162nd DEP BRIG to 9-14-1918, with Camp Pike SEPT AUT REPL DRAFT Co., 12th Infantry to 10-11-1918, with Co. B, 161st Infantry to 10-22-1918, and with Co. F, 23rd Infantry until his discharge. He served overseas from 9-26-1918 to 8-03-1919. (Missouri Digital Heritage)

He departed from Hoboken, New Jersey on 9-20-1918 aboard the *Northern Pacific*. He departed for home on 7-23-1919 from Brest, France aboard the *Virginian*. (www.ancestry.com)

AUDA DOIL RUSH

Born 1-01-1899 – Died 9-29-1957

He was buried at White Chapel Memorial Gardens in Wichita, KS. He was the son of Charles Franklin Rush and Polly Ann (Pool) Rush and was married to Evelyn Demarious (Denney) Rush. (findagrave.com)

According to his World War I Draft Registration card, he was of medium height and build and had dark brown hair and blue eyes. (www.ancestry.com)

GEORGE C. SAMUELS, PVT., US ARMY

Born 6-05-1895 – Died 11-21-1968

He was buried in the Seymour Masonic Cemetery. He was the son of Robert B. Samuels and Minerva Elizabeth (Conn) Samuels and was married to Annie (Blevins) Samuels. According to his World War I Draft Registration card, he was short, of medium build, and had red hair and light blue eyes. (www.ancestry.com)

He enlisted on 4-26-1918 and was discharged on 6-05-1919. He served in Co. B, 340th MG BN. He departed for home from Brest, France on 5-15-1919 aboard the *Leviathan* and arrived in Hoboken, New Jersey on 5-22-1919. (www.ancestry.com)

ISAAC NEWTON SANDERS, US ARMY/MARINE

Born 6-16-1890 – Died 4-2-1957

He was buried at Clever Creek Cemetery in Douglas County, MO. He was married to Mary Elizabeth (Smith) Sanders. (findagrave.com)

He was inducted at Ava, MO on 9-18-1917 and served with Battery C, 342nd Field Artillery. He was overseas from 6-28-1918 to 5-27-1919. (Missouri Digital Heritage)

WILLIAM RICHARD SCHLICHER, PVT. 1st CLASS, US ARMY/MARINE

Born 7-31-1895 – Died 9-11-1961 in Wichita, KS

He was buried at White Chapel Memorial Gardens in Wichita, KS. He was the son of Charles Schlicher and Lora Ann "Annie" (Hord) Schlicher who were buried in Macomb Cemetery. He was married to Mary Ann (Schoos) Schlicher. (findagrave.com)

He was residing in Macomb, MO when he departed from Hoboken, New Jersey on 5-02-

1918 aboard the *Great Northern* and served in Co. B, 110th Regiment Engineers. He departed for home on 4-11-1919 from Brest, France aboard the *Von Steuben* and arrived in Hoboken, New Jersey on 4-19-1919. According to his World War I Draft Registration card, he was of medium height and build and had black hair and brown eyes. (www.ancestry.com)

JAMES BRODIE SCOTT, PVT., US ARMY/MARINE

Born 10-06-1894 – Died 10-06-1918

He was buried in Fowler Cemetery in Texas County, MO. He was the son of James L. Scott and Clementina Scott. (findagrave.com)

He was inducted at Houston, MO, on 7-25-1918 and was assigned to Co. 23, 164th DEP BRIG to 8-10-1918 and to Co. A, 70th Infantry until his death. (Missouri Digital Heritage)

He departed from New York on 8-09-1918 aboard the *Olympic*. He was assigned to Construction Company Bricklaying No 11.

He died of lobar pneumonia; his wife, Blanche Scott, of Fowler, MO was notified of his death. (Missouri Digital Heritage)

According to his World War I Draft Registration card, he was single, of medium height and build and had light brown hair and light brown eyes. (www.ancestry.com)

CLIFFORD MARKMUS SEAL, PVT. 1st CLASS, US ARMY/MARINE

Born 2-16-1891 – Died 6-28-1978

He was buried in Tracy Public Cemetery in Tracy, CA. He was the son of John Elbert Seal and Martha Elizabeth (Moles) Seal, who were buried in the Mansfield Cemetery. He was married to Ollie Opal Seal. (findagrave.com)

He was inducted in Hartville, MO, on 10-02-1917. He was overseas from 5-20-1918 to 4-20-1919. (Missouri Digital Heritage)

He departed from NYC on 5-20-1918 aboard the *Saxonia*. He was a Private First Class and served with HQ Co., 129th Field Artillery, 35th Division. He departed for home on 4-09-1919 from Brest, France aboard the *Zeppelin* and arrived in Hoboken, New Jersey on 4-20-1919. (www.ancestry.com)

According to his World War I Draft Registration card, he was short, of medium build, and had dark brown hair and blue eyes. (www.ancestry.com)

ELMER OLIVER SELLERS, CPL., US ARMY

Born 8-28-1894 – Died 10-21-1918 in France

He was buried in the Meuse-Argonne American Cemetery in Romagne, France. He was the son of John J. Sellers and Alice Cordelia (Tindall) Sellers. (findagrave.com)

He was inducted at Ava, MO, on 9-08-1917. He was a member of BTRY C, 342nd Field Artillery, 307th Infantry Regiment, 77th Division. (Missouri Digital Heritage)

He departed from New York on 8-08-1918 aboard the *Otranto*. (www.ancestry.com)

He was awarded the Purple Heart. (HonorStates.org)

ORA (ORON) SHERRELL, PVT., US ARMY/MARINE

Born 12-14-1891 – Died 4-03-1933

He was buried in Hillcrest Cemetery in Mountain Grove, MO. He was the son of Thomas Fielding Sherrell and Louisa S. (Ousley) Sherrell and was married to Grace E. (Herrin) Sherrell Nelson. (findagrave.com)

He was inducted in Ozark, MO on 5-28-1918 and served in Co. F, 350th Infantry. He served overseas from 8-11-1918 to 5-30-1919. (Missouri Digital Heritage)

He departed from Brooklyn, New York on 8-11-1918 aboard the *Delta*. He departed for home on 8-19-1919 from St. Nazaire, France aboard the *Aeolus* and arrived at Camp Alexander in Newport News, VA. According to his World War I Draft Registration card, he was of medium height and build and had dark brown hair and brown eyes. (www.ancestry.com)

HERBERT ANESWORTH SHORT, HS., US ARMY

Born 5-4-1894 – Died 7-26-1979

He was buried in the Mansfield Cemetery, Mansfield, MO. He was the son of Elmer Elsworth Short and Rebecca Ann (Moore) Short and was married to Nellie Blanche (Bolender) Short. (findagrave.com)

He was inducted at Hartville, MO on 10-02-1917. (Missouri Digital Heritage)

He departed from New York on 6-12-1918 aboard the *Carpathia*. He served as a Horseshoer Engineer with the 314th Engineer Train, 89th Division. He returned to the U.S. aboard the *Harrisburg* from Brest, France on 5-15-1919 and was expected to arrive in Hoboken, New Jersey, eight days later. He was discharged on 6-09-1919. According to his World War I Draft Registration card, he was of medium height and build and had dark hair and blue eyes. (www.ancestry.com)

JASON SHUMATE, US ARMY/MARINE

Born 5-31-1892 – Died 11-06-1958 in Mansfield

He was buried in White Chapel Memorial Gardens in Springfield, MO. He was the son of John C. Shumate and Clara Helen (Wigginton) Shumate, who lived in Wright County, and was married to Laura Ethel (Newton) Shumate in 1913. (findagrave.com)

According to his World War I Draft Registration card, he was of medium height and build and had dark brown hair and light blue eyes. (www.ancestry.com)

WILLIAM EVERETT SIKES

Born 12-16-1896 in Mansfield – Died 10-08-1962 in Fresno, CA

He was buried in Deep Creek Cemetery in Farmersville, CA. He was the son of William Alexander Sikes and Mary Elizabeth (Forbes) Sikes and married Della Pearl (Toles) Sikes. He enlisted on 8-28-1918 and served in Co. I, 330th Infantry Qmc. He was discharged on 10-29-1919. (findagrave.com)

According to his World War I Draft Registration card, he was tall, of medium build and had brown hair and gray eyes. (www.ancestry.com)

JAMES K. POLK SKELTON, PVT., US ARMY

Born 1892 – Died 7-17-1918 in France

He was buried in Weaver Chapel Cemetery in Hatfield, Mo. The inscription on his tombstone reads "CO L 4th Inf USA WWI." He was the son of James Edward Skelton and Rebecca Jane (Stephenson) Skelton. (findagrave.com)

He was inducted at Bethany, MO on 10-02-1917 and served with Co. B, 356th Infantry to 2-26-1918 and with Co. L 4 Infantry until his death. He served overseas from 5-21-1918 to 7-17-1918. He died from wounds received in action; his father, James Skelton of Hatfield, MO was notified of his death. (Missouri Digital Heritage)

He was awarded the Purple Heart and the World War I Victory Medal. (HonorStates.org)

JAMES WARREN SKILES, PVT., US ARMY

Born 3-09-1887 – Died 9-30-1918 in France

He was buried in Hillcrest Cemetery in Mountain Grove, MO. He was the son of Francis M. and Mary E. Skiles.

He enlisted as a private at Nevada, MO on 9-20-1917. He departed from Hoboken, New Jersey on 9-26-1918 aboard the *Great Northern* and served overseas from 5-27-1918 until his death in September. He died in the Meuse-Argonne Offensive in France in WWI. He belonged to Company F, 140th Infantry, 35th Div. He was the recipient (assumed posthumously) of the Victory Medal, Defensive Sector, and the Meuse-Argonne clasps. (Missouri Digital Heritage)

He also received the Purple Heart. (HonorStates.org)

He was transported home on 2-11-1919 from St. Nazaire, France aboard the *Huron* and arrived at Newport News, Virginia. According to his World War I Draft Registration card, he was slender, of medium height and had light-colored hair and blue eyes. (www.ancestry.com)

GEORGE O. "OLA" SMITH, PVT., US ARMY

Born 10-12-1896 – Died 8-08-1918 in France

He was buried in Smith Cemetery #01 in Seymour, MO. The inscriptions on his tombstone read, "Died in France for the sake of his country" and "Ammunition Train 117th." He was the son of James Henry Smith and Martha Ann "Mattie" (Jenkins) Smith. (findagrave.com)

He departed from Hoboken, New Jersey on 10-29-1917 aboard the *America*. He served with Caisson Co. #1. (www.ancestry.com)

He died of wounds received in action. He was awarded the Purple Heart. (HonorStates.org)

OWEN LEWIS SMITH, CPL., US ARMY/ MARINE

Born 8-06-1892 – Died 12-13-1959

He was buried in Eureka, Greenwood County, KS. He was the son of William Robert Smith and Hannah (Chambers) Smith and was married to Edith Mae Teegardin. (findagrave.com)

He was inducted at Hartville, MO on 5-28-1918 and served with Co. F, 350th Infantry. He served overseas from 8-11-1918 to 5-30-1919. (Missouri Digital Heritage)

ROBERT SMITH, PVT., US ARMY

Born 11-08-1894 – Died 10-07-1918

He was buried in Brixey Cemetery in Seymour, MO. He was the son of Joseph Sigel Smith and Jessie Mary (Moore) Poole. (findagrave.com)

He was inducted at Seymour, MO on 5-28-1918 and served with Co. F, 350th Infantry, 88th Division. He served overseas from 8-11-1918 to 10-07-1918. He died from pneumonia; his mother, Mrs. Jesse Hurd of Seymour, MO, was notified of his death. (Missouri Digital Heritage)

He was awarded the World War I Victory Medal. (HonorStates.org)

HENRY ISAAC SNOW, PVT., US ARMY/ MARINE

Born 4-11-1897 – Died 10-09-1918

He was buried in the McBride Cemetery, in Competition, MO. He was the son of George Washington Snow and Amanda E. "Mandy" Snow. (findagrave.com)

He was inducted at Hartville, MO on 7-25-1918. He served in 22 Co., 164th DEP BRIG, and then in Co. A, 70th Infantry. He died of lobar pneumonia; Oliver Snow of Grovespring, MO was notified of his death. (Missouri Digital Heritage)

JOHN "ERNIE" ERNEST SPURLOCK, COOK, US ARMY/MARINE

Born 7-21-1894 – Died 1-19-1978

He was buried at Collins Cemetery in Story County, Iowa. He was the son of Judge John Andrew "John A" Spurlock and Cynthia Jane "Jennie" (Huffman) Spurlock and was married to Fern Hazel (Bloomfield) Spurlock.(findagrave.com)

He was inducted at Ava, MO on 6-27-1917 and was 22 11/12ths years old. He served in Supply Co., 6th Infantry NG and then in Supply Co., 140th Infantry. He served overseas from 4-26-1918 to 1-23-1919 and was discharged with a 20% disability. (Missouri Digital Heritage)

He departed from Brooklyn, New York on 4-25-1918 aboard the *Shropshire*. He served as a cook in Supply Co., 140th Infantry, 35th Division. He departed for home on 1-10-1919 from St. Nazaire, France on the *Manchuria*. He arrived at Hoboken, New Jersey on 1-22-1919. According to his World War I Draft Registration card, he was of medium height and build and had light brown hair and gray eyes. (www.ancestry.com)

(Information courtesy of Randy Spurlock)

HARRY B. STEPHENS, CPL., US ARMY/MARINE

He was inducted at Columbus, OH on 5-11-1917. He served overseas from 1-19-1918 to 1-07-1919 with the 17th Aero-Squadron. (Missouri Digital Heritage)

In the 1920 Missouri Census he was listed as 24 years old and living with his brother Mark in Wright County, MO.

IRA CLARENCE STOUT, COOK, US ARMY/MARINE

Born 2-26-1893 – Died 9-27-1955

He was buried in Exeter District Cemetery in Exeter, Ca. He was the son of Jonathan Ela Stout and Sarah Jane (Hicks) Stout. (findagrave.com)

He was inducted at Hartville, MO on 10-2-1917 and served with Co. C, 314th Engineers to 1-05-1918, BTRY B, 341st Field Artillery to 9-01-1918, and HQ Company 341st Field Artillery until discharge. He was overseas from 6-28-1918 to 5-24-1919. (Missouri Digital Heritage)

ELMER STRONG, PVT., US ARMY/MARINE

Born 1-14-1891 – Died 8-04-1955

He was buried in White Chapel Memorial Gardens in Springfield, MO. He was the son of James Monroe Strong and Nancy Parnell and was married to Jessie (Brasher) Strong. (findagrave.com)

He was inducted in Wright County on 8-14-1918 and was a member of MTC REPAIR UNIT 316. (Missouri Digital Heritage)

LESTER RAY SUTHERLAND, PVT., US ARMY/MARINE

Born 6-15-1893 – Died 12-03-1917

He was buried at Denlow Cemetery in Douglas County, MO. He was the son of William Franklin Sutherland and Neta Arada "Rady" (Souder) Sutherland. The remains of Lester Sutherland, who died from pneumonia, arrived from Camp Funston and were sent to the home of his parents near Cold Springs, MO. (findagrave.com)

He was inducted at Ava, MO on 9-18-1917 and served with BTRY C, 342nd Field Artillery TO; TR B 314 MP until his death. He died of broncho pneumonia; his mother, Arada Sutherland of Cold Springs, MO, was notified of his death. (Missouri Digital Heritage)

CLYDE TARBUTTON, WAG., US ARMY/MARINE

Born 12-06-1895 – Died 7-20-1966

He was buried in the Mansfield Cemetery in Mansfield, MO. He was the son of William Henry Tarbutton and Lula Ann (Wells) Tarbutton and was married to Eulalia (Tripp) Tarbutton. (findagrave.com)

He was inducted at Seymour, MO on 7-26-1917 and served overseas as a wagoner in Supply Co., 6th Infantry, NG Missouri. He served overseas from 4-25-1918 to 4-28-1919. (Missouri Digital Heritage)

He departed for home from St. Nazaire, France on 4-15-1919 aboard the *Nansemond*. (www.ancestry.com)

According to his World War I Draft Registration card, he was short, of medium build, and had dark brown hair and brown eyes. (www.ancestry.com)

W.F.C. Clyde Tarbutton enlisted in April 1917 and served with Supply Co., 140th Infantry, 35th Division. He trained at Fort Sill, OK and embarked in May 1918. His engagements included the St. Mihiel, Meuse-Argonne, and Verdun Battles. He returned to the United States in April 1919 and was discharged in May 1919. (Clarence King Post American Legion's *Service Record Book*)

JAMES TEFTELLER, PVT., US ARMY/ MARINE

Born 7-18-1886 – Died 8-5-1973 in Tulare, CA

He was buried at Prairie Hollow Cemetery in Douglas County, MO. He was the son of Marcellus Manvel "Marsh" Tefteller and Hulda Jane (England) Tefteller and was married to Alice Viola (Gann) Tefteller. (findagrave.com)

He was attached to Battery A, 340th FANA, 89th Div. According to his World War I Draft Registration card, he was short, of medium build, and had dark brown hair and blue eyes. (www.ancestry.com)

LEON RAYMOND TESTER, PVT., US ARMY

Born 5-01-1896 - Died 10-02-1918 in France

He was buried in Little Creek Cemetery in Hartville, MO. He was the son of John William Tester and Mellissa Tester. (findagrave.com)

He was inducted at Hartville, MO on 10-02-1917. He served overseas from 5-20-1918 to 10-02-1918. He was a member of 7th Co., 164th DEP BRIG from 10-02-1917 to 10-23-1917 and of BTRY D, 128th FA to 10-02-1918. His father, John, of Grove Spring, MO was notified that his son was killed in action. (Missouri Digital Heritage)

He was awarded the Purple Heart and the World War I Victory Medal. (HonorStates.org)

MAYNARD HALL THORNE, SGT., US ARMY/MARINE

Born 12-26-1892 – Died 10-15-1918

He was buried at Hillcrest Cemetery in Mountain Grove, MO. He was married to Nelle Jeanette (Myers) Coulter. (findagrave.com)

He was inducted at Hartville on 7-15-1918. He served in Co. A, 7th REPL TNG BN until his death. He died of broncho pneumonia, and his mother, Anna Thorne, of Marmaduke, MO was notified of his death. (Missouri Digital Heritage)

JOSEPH CLARENCE TODD, CPL., US ARMY

Born 8-25-1896 – Died 4-04-1983

He was buried in Coon Creek Cemetery in Wright County, MO. He was the son of Robert Preston Todd and Eliza Ann (Barnes) Todd and was married to Martha Emma Almeda Todd. (findagrave.com)

He departed for home on 11-22-1920 from Antwerp, Belgium aboard the *Pocahontas*, arriving in Hoboken, New Jersey on 12-08-1920. He was a member of Co. B 1 ENG.

According to his World War I Draft Registration card, he was tall, of medium build, and had brown hair and gray eyes. (www.ancestry.com). He was awarded the World War I Victory Medal. (HonorStates.org)

JOSEPH MAURICE TODD, PVT., US ARMY

Born 7-07-1895 - Died 10-10-1918

He was inducted at Hartville, MO on 3-04-1918. He served overseas from 8-23-1918 to 10-10-1918. He was a member of HQ CAS DET MOTC MED DEPT at Fort Riley, KS from 3-04-1918 to 4-23-1918; Cooks & Bakers School MOTC at Fort Riley, KS to 5-11-1918; Hospital Train 39 MOTC at Fort Riley to 7-03-1918; HQ CAS DET MOTC at Fort Riley to 7-09-1918; B H 58 Camp Grant, IL to 10-10-1918. He died of pneumonia, and his brother, Martin V. Todd, of Grove Springs, MO was notified. (Missouri Digital Heritage)

He departed from New York on 8-23-1918 aboard the *Chicago*. According to his World War I Draft Registration card, he was of medium height and build and had black hair and light brown eyes. (www.ancestry.com)

He was awarded the World War I Victory Medal. (HonorStates.org)

ARCHIE WALTER TOOL, US ARMY/ MARINE

Born 2-16-1888 – Died 12-04-1918

He was buried in Hensley Cemetery near Mansfield, MO. He was the son of Oscar Nelson Stinson Tool and Lydia Araminda Tool. (findagrave.com)

He served with Bakers and Cooks (Wisconsin Veterans WWI Roster Database). He died at Camp Hancock, GA, and his body was shipped to Mansfield. A short service was held at the cemetery, conducted by Rev. T. B. Ritzinger. (findagrave.com)

According to his World War I Draft Registration card, he was tall, slender, and had dark brown hair and blue eyes. (www.ancestry.com)

ROY WILLIAM TOOLEY, PVT., US ARMY

Born 11-16-1895 – Died 11-04-1918 in France

He was buried in the Vanzant Cemetery in Vanzant, MO. He was the son of Tandy Doss Tooley and Nora Amanda (Knight) Tooley.

He was inducted at Ava, MO on 7-15-1918 and left from Hoboken, NJ on the *Leviathan* to serve with the September Automatic Replacement Draft Co., 29th Infantry at Camp McArthur, TX. (www.ancestry.com)

He was killed in action just eight days before the armistice was signed and less than four months after leaving home. It is believed that he was the first Douglas County boy to die in the war; his father, Doss T. Tooley of Vanzant, MO, was notified of his death. (findagrave.com)

He was awarded the Purple Heart and the World War I Victory Medal. (HonorStates.org)

CLAUDE ELMER TRIPP, WAG., US ARMY/MARINE

Born 9-13-1894 – Died 1-10-1957

He was buried in the Mansfield Cemetery. He was the son of George Washington Tripp and Laura Emiline (Newton) Tripp and was married to Rhoda Ann (Taylor) Tripp. (findagrave.com)

He was inducted at Seymour, MO on 7-25-1917 at 21 ¾ years old. He served overseas as a wagoner with Supply Co., 6th Infantry and with Supply Co., 140th Infantry, 35th Division. (Missouri Digital Heritage)

He departed from Brooklyn, NY on 4-25-1918 aboard the *Shropshire*. (www.ancestry.com)

According to his World War I Draft Registration card, he was short, stout, and had black hair and brown eyes. (www.ancestry.com)

ORLANDO KARL TRIPP, US ARMY/MARINE

Born 2-3-1894 – Died 11-23-1986

He was buried in the Mansfield Cemetery. He was the son of Samuel Tripp (born in England) and Elizabeth Ann (Rosevear) Tripp and was married to Eula Edith (Newton) Tripp. (findagrave.com)

He was inducted at Hartville on 7-25-1918 and served with HQ Co. 70th Infantry. (Missouri Digital Heritage)

According to his World War I Draft Registration card, he was tall, stout, and had brown hair and light blue eyes. (www.ancestry.com)

ALVA MCKINLEY TURNER, PVT., US ARMY

Born 8-15-1896 – Died 8-30-1968

He was buried in the Mansfield Cemetery in Mansfield, MO. He was the son of J. C. Turner and Ava L. Turner. He enlisted at Hartville, MO on 8-27-1918 and served with the 164th DEP BRIG to 10-24-1918 and Co. K, 41st Infantry until his discharge on 2-25-1919. (Missouri Digital Heritage)

He served at Camp Funston, KS and was discharged on 2-25-1919. (Clarence King Post American Legion's *Service Record Book*)

According to his World War I Draft Registration card, he was slender, tall, and had black hair and brown eyes. (www.ancestry.com)

CARL RAYMOND TURNER, US ARMY/MARINE

Born 3-18-1893 – Died 9-10-1957

He was buried at Hensley Cemetery in Wright County, MO. He was the son of Jesse Andrew Turner and Sarah Jane (Hensley) Turner and was married to Carrie Turner. (findagrave.com)

According to his World War I Draft Registration card, he was married and lived in Wright County, MO. He was short, of medium build, and had brown hair and light blue eyes. (www.ancestry.com)

He was inducted at Saint Louis, MO on 6-24-1918 and served with the 162nd DEP BRIG to 9-07-1918, Co. F, 4th TNG REGT Camp Pike, AR, and Co. H, 108th Infantry. He served overseas from 10-25-1918 to 3-06-1919. (Missouri Digital Heritage)

ROBERT C. VILES, PVT., US ARMY/MARINE

Born 7-30-1900 – Died 12-7-1938

He was buried in Crown Hill Cemetery in Wheat Ridge, Colorado. He was the son of Voler V. Viles and Jessie P. (Gorman) Viles, who were residents of Mansfield, MO. (findagrave.com)

He enlisted at Mansfield Supply Co. but was underaged. He was later inducted on 10-29-1918 in Washington, DC. and served with Motor Company 2 MTC at Camp Johnston, Florida. (www.ancestry.com)

CLAUDE FLORAN WALLACE, APPRENTICE SEAMAN, U.S. NAVY

Born 5-17-1900 – Died 1-26-1918

He lived in Basher, MO. He was buried in Dyer Cemetery in Douglas County, MO. The footstone at the cemetery shows his date of death as 1-19-1918. He was the son of George Franklin Wallace and Sarah Elizabeth "Bettie" (Lewis) Wallace. (findagrave.com)

He enlisted at the recruiting station in Kansas City, MO. He served at the Naval Training Station in Great Lakes, IL from 12-16-1917 to 1-26-1918 when he entered the Naval Hospital in Great Lakes, IL. (Missouri Digital Heritage)

His cause of death was broncho-pneumonia; his father, George Wallace of Basher, MO, was notified of his death. (www.ancestry.com)

ROBERT REED WHITTEKER, WAG., US ARMY/MARINE/NATIONAL GUARD

Born 5-25-1896 – Died 8-27-1986

He was buried in the Steele Memorial Cemetery in Hartville, MO. He was the son of Amanda Jane Whitteker Moody and was married to Della (Gregory) Whitteker. (findagrave.com)

He was inducted at Seymour, MO on 6-21-1917 at 20 11/12 years old. He served as a wagoner with Supply Co., 6th Infantry, Missouri NG and with Supply Co., 140th Infantry, 35th Div. He was overseas from 4-25-1918 to 4-28-1919. (Missouri Digital Heritage)

He departed from Brooklyn, New York on 4-25-1918 aboard the *Shropshire*. He departed for home on 4-15-1919 from St. Nazaire, France aboard the *Nansemond*. According to his World War I Draft Registration card, he was tall, slender, and had black hair and brown eyes. (www.ancestry.com)

JAMES ILA WILLIAMS, PVT. 1st Class, US ARMY/MARINE

Born 10-21-1894 – Died 7-17-1988

He was buried in Memorial Park Cemetery in Tulsa, OK. He was the son of Andrew Newton Williams and Lucinda (Smith) Williams. (findagrave.com)

He was inducted at Ava, MO on 9-18-1917 and served with Battery C, 342nd Field Artillery. He was overseas from 6-28-1918 to 5-27-1919. (Missouri Digital Heritage)

He departed from New York on 6-28-1918 aboard the *Justicia*. He departed for home on 5-18-1919 from Brest, France aboard the *Prinz Friedrich Wilhelm* and arrived in Hoboken, New Jersey on 5-27-1919.

According to his World War I Draft Registration card, he was of medium height, slender, and had light brown hair and light blue eyes. (www.ancestry.com)

WILLIAM OLIVER WOODFORD, PVT., US ARMY

Born 6-07-1888 – Died 10-18-1918 in France

He was buried in Mount Tabor Cemetery in Douglas County, MO. He was the son of J. D. Woodford and Elizabeth "Lizzie" (Edwards) DeWeese. (findagrave.com)

He was inducted at Ava, MO on 5-28-1918 and served with the 163rd DEP BRIG to 6-04-1918 and Co. G, 350th Infantry until his death. He departed from New York on 8-15-1918 aboard the *Kashmir*. He died of broncho pneumonia; his mother, Lizzie Deweese of Arno, MO, was notified of his death. (Missouri Digital Heritage)

According to his World War I Draft Registration card, he was short, slender, and had light brown hair and gray eyes. (www.ancestry.com).
He was awarded the World War I Victory Medal. (HonorStates.org)

FRANK ANSON WRIGHT, MECH, US ARMY

Born 1-05-1893 – Died 2-24-1919 in France

He was buried in Pleasant View Cemetery in Montrose, KS. He was the son of George Clifton Wright and Irena Jane (Anson) Wright of Mountain Grove, MO and was married to Elsa M. (Shackelton) Wright. (findagrave.com)

He was drafted on 10-03-1917 and sent to Camp Funston to join the 140th Depot Brigade, Co. B. At Camp Kearney he was transferred to Co. B, 160th Infantry. He left Brooklyn, New York on 8-08-1918 aboard the *Mentor*. He was a Private First Class mechanic. After a two month illness, he passed away. According to his World War I Draft Registration card, he was of medium build, tall, and had light brown hair and blue eyes. (www.ancestry.com)

OTIS YEAGER, PVT., US ARMY/MARINE

Born 11-28-1896 – Died 10-07-1918

He was buried in Coon Creek Cemetery in Hartville, Missouri. He was the son of Robert Lee Yeager and Edith Eliza (Stacy) Yeager. (findagrave.com)

He was inducted at Hartville, MO on 8-27-1918. He was a member of 17 Co., 164th DEP BRIG to 9-20-1918 and of Co. G, 20th Infantry until his death. He died of lobar pneumonia. His mother, Mrs. Edith Yeager, was notified. (Missouri Digital Heritage)

According to his World War I Draft Registration card, he was tall, of medium build, and had dark brown hair and blue eyes. (www.ancestry.com)

He was awarded the World War I Victory Medal. (HonorStates.org)

FLOYD S. YOUNG, PVT., US ARMY

Born May 1896 – Died 11-02-1918 in France

He was buried in Arlington National Cemetery in Arlington, VA. He was the son of Edward Levi Young and Lillie Christie (Dunham) and was married to Clara Cathaleen (Taber) Wadlow.

According to his World War I Draft Registration card, he was of medium height and build and had brown hair and blue eyes. (familysearch.org)

He was inducted at Farmington, MO on 2-25-1918 He served in Co. 27, 164th DEP BRIG from 2-25-1918 to 3-28-1918, with the 341st Field Artillery to 4-12-1918, and with Battery F, 341st Field Artillery to 11-02-1918. He served overseas from 6-22-1918 to 11-02-1918. He died of pneumonia; his wife, Mrs. Clara Young, of Bunker, MO was notified of his death. (Missouri Digital Heritage)

He received the World War I Victory Medal. (HonorStates.org)

IRA ELMER YOUNG, PFC., US ARMY/MARINE (Older brother of Raymond Young)

Born 4-07-1893 – Died 7-28-1946

He was buried at the Golden Gate National Cemetery in San Bruno, CA. He was the son of Alford Locratus Young and Mary Adeline Young and was married to Nettie Villeta Young. (findagrave.com)

He was inducted at Hartville, MO on 10-01-1917. He served overseas from 5-20-1918 to 1-19-1919. He was a member of 164th DEP BRIG to 10-23-17 and 163rd DEP BRIG to his discharge. (Missouri Digital Heritage)

He departed from New York on 5-20-1918 aboard the *Saxonia*. He was a Private First Class in Battery D, 128th Field Artillery, 35th Division. He departed for home from Bordeaux, France on 1-06-1919 aboard the *Wilhelmina* and arrived in Hoboken, New Jersey on 1-19-1919. He was listed in the Bordeaux Casual Company No.12. (www.ancestry.com)

According to his World War I Draft Registration card, he was tall, of medium build, and had light brown hair and blue eyes. (www.ancestry.com)

JESSE ALLEN YOUNG, PVT. 1st CLASS, US ARMY

Died 11-10-1894 – Died 11-23-1966

He was buried in Pleasant Hill Cemetery in Hartville, MO. He was the son of Reuben Young and Sarah Alice (Miller) Young and was married to Ava Louvela (Jones) Young. (findagrave.com)

He enlisted at Hartville, MO on 7-25-1918 and served with the 164th DEP BRIG to 8-10-1918 and then Co. A, 70th Infantry until his discharge. (Missouri Digital Heritage)

According to his World War I Draft Registration card, he was of medium height and build and had dark brown hair and light brown eyes. He was discharged on 2-04-1919. (www.ancestry.com)

RAY YOUNG, BUGLER, US ARMY/ MARINE

Born – Died 11-01-1918

He was buried in the Pleasant Hill Cemetery. He was the son of James Young and Liza A. Young of Hartville. (findagrave.com)

He was inducted at Fort Logan, CO. on 1-20-1916 and served with Co. G, 1st Infantry as a bugler. He died of broncho pneumonia; his mother, Liza A. Young, was notified of his death. (Missouri Digital Heritage)

RAYMOND YOUNG, PVT., US ARMY/ MARINE (Younger brother of Ira Young)

Born 3-18-1896 – Died 6-25-1968

He was buried in Turlock Memorial Park in Turlock, CA. He was the son of Alford Locratus Young and Mary Adeline Young and was married to Lillie Mary (McLaughlin) Young. (findagrave.com)

He was inducted at Hartville, MO on 5-28-1918. He was a member of Co. F, 350th Infantry and served overseas from 8-11-1918 to 5-22-1919. He was 10% disabled. (Missouri Digital Heritage)

He departed for home from St. Nazaire, France on 5-22-1919 aboard the *Manchuria* and arrived in Hoboken, New Jersey. He was a private in the Infantry and was reported to be sick and wounded. (www.ancestry.com)

According to his World War I Draft Registration card, he was tall, of medium build, and had light brown hair and blue eyes. (www.ancestry.com)

THE MANSFIELD AREA HISTORICAL SOCIETY

The members of the Mansfield Area Historical Society have long felt a need to preserve the historical significance of this area. The authors, whose families have lived here for generations, have compiled these writings and images from their own collections, from local residents, and from online resources.

The Mansfield Area Historical Museum is a non-profit, volunteer-driven organization that is open free to the public Monday through Saturday from 10:00 AM to 12:00 PM and from 1:00 PM to 4:00 PM. Donations are appreciated.

For additional information, you can contact the Mansfield Area Historical Society on Facebook or call us at 417-924-4041.

INDEX

(**Ded.** Refers to the Dedication page; **Ack.** refers to the Acknowledgements page; **Notes** refers to Notes to the Reader; **Intro.** refers to the Introduction)

Akers, Homer John	...27, 96, 101
Akers, Mrs. Leona	...27, 68
Akers, Walter Jackson (POW)	...27, 38, 39, 101
Alsup, John Benton "Jack"	...101
Baker, Pvt. Ova "Ovie" Elijah	...95, 102
Ball, Charles "Charlie" Austin	...Ded., 102
Ball, Pvt. Palmer French	...Ded., 102
Bare, Pvt. Roy Wesley	...Ded., 103
Bass, Pvt. Orean Harvey	...103
Bausch, James John	...103
Beach, Pvt. Charles Walter	...51, 104
Beckett, Pvt. Frank	...Ded., 104
Berry, Maurice S.	...104
Binkley, Pvt. Henry Otto F.	...Ded., 104
Blankenship, Vicki	...Ack.
Borders, Sherman Winfield	...40, 91, 105
Bragg, Harley W.	...Ded., 111
Branstetter, Pvt. James Marion	...Ded., 105
Brasher, William "Willie" Henry	...106
Brazeal, Cpl. Jesse	...Ded., 106
Breckner, Pvt. Lloyd Daniel	...Ded., 106
Brentlinger, Charlie	...52
Briggs, Franklin Oliver	...5, 106
Brophy, Cpl. Joseph Hillary	...107
Brown, Pvt. Charles A.	...107
Brown, Henry Oscar	...13, 107
Brown, Pvt. Ira Chelsea	...108
Brown, Pvt. James Madison	...108
Burks (Burk), Pvt. Delbert	...108
Butzke, Ernest J.	...51
Cameron, James	...83
Canifax, John William	...74, 108
Carrick, Pfc. Raymond	...5, 109
Carter, Alva	...5, 6, 51
Carter, Pvt. Charles Thomas	...Ded., 109
Carter, Sgt. Garrett William "China"	...5, 6, 51, 94, 109
Carter, John Alva	...5, 110
Chadwell, Pvt. James C.	...Ded., 110
Chapman, Ralph Hoyt	...111
Cher Ami	...58, 59
Clark, Cpl. Alexander	...Ded., 111
Clark, Pvt. Claude Noble	...112
Claxton, Howard Noah	...5, 6, 112
Claxton, Pvt. James "Tiny" Anderson	...91, 112

Coday, Berlin	…81, 112
Coday, Herve E.	…39
Coday, Sgt. Walter Clay	…5, 6, 40, 51, 71, 94, 95, 113
Collins, Pvt. Monroe W.	…113
Cornett, Pvt. Willie M.	…113
Craig, William Glen	…5, 6, 9, 52, 94, 113
Crippen, Pvt. Earnie Nicholas	…48, 74, 95, 114
Crisp, Pvt. Jess S.	…Ded., 114
Crouch, James B.	…114
Crowder, Enoch	…68
Curtis, Pvt William "Jack" Coleman	…114
Dake, Pvt. Ralph Raymond	…35, 91, 115
Davidson, Pvt. Lon	…115
Davis, Pvt. "Bob/Bobbie"	…31, 95, 115
Davis, Jesse Elmer	…116
Davis, John	…20
Davis, Oren Linzy	…116
Denney, Pvt. Curtis Kelly	…81, 116
Dennis, Cpl. Frank Alva	…116
Dennis, J. Lon	…94
Dennis, Joe H.	…44, 45
Dennis, Pvt. Marvin Hanks	…21, 37, 40, 43, 44, 45, 91, 95, 116
Dennis, Ural Raphael	…44, 117
Denny, William W.	…5
Denton, Pvt. Oscar Alonzo	…Ded., 117
Dodson, Morgan Edwin	…117
Duckworth, Ann	…Ack.
Duckworth, Pvt. James Alfred	…79, 118
Dudley, John Foster, Sr.	…118
Edens, 1st Lt. Louis Martin (POW)	…38, 96, 118
Edwards, Pvt. Glen Hobart	…Ded., 118
Elliott, Pvt. Edgar Lee	…119
Ellis, Pvt. David Stone	…119
Ely, Seaman 1st Class Lee	…120
Evans, Pvt. Joseph Franklin	…Ded., 120
Ferdinand, Archduke Franz	…Notes
Ferrell, Pvt. Clifford Earl	…5, 120
Findley, Pvt. George Elmer	…3, 120
Findley, Pvt. James Harve	…121
Floyd, Pfc. Samuel David	…Ded., 121
Foster, Pvt. John William Earl	…122
Freeman, Pvt. George Burney	…122
Freeman, G. C.	…68
Freeman, Joseph Alva	…122
Freeman, Pvt. Willie	…122
Fritz, Pvt. Ray Lerone	…123
Fry, Pvt. Charles Howard	…123
Fry, Evans	…123
Fry, Wesley Woodard	…123
Gartin, Alva	…Ded., 123
Gaskill, Clella	…21
Gaskill, Enoch Preston	…124
Gaskill, Pvt. Ernest Elwood	…10, 15, 40, 42, 91, 124

Gaskill, Evan Dea	…52, 124
Gaskill, Pvt. George Washington	…50, 125
Gaskill, Stella	…10
Gilley, J. W.	…Intro., 85
Gilley, Seaman 2nd Class Earl Raymond	…45, 95, 125
Goss, Kay Dunnegan	…26, 27, 63
Greenwood, William Richard	…39, 125
Gresham, Seaman 2nd Class Paul Edwin	…Ded., 126
Handy, Roy L.	…5, 6, 9, 94, 95, 126
Hassler, Orran L.	…126
Hays, Harry	…51
Heatherly, Pvt. Lewis Walter	…127
Helsley, Hershel	…79
Helsley, Sherman	…78, 79
Hensley, Clarence Edward	…15, 127
Hensley, Roscoe C.	…62, 127
Hensley, Pvt. Roy L.	…72, 73, 128
Henson, Carl McKinley	…82, 95, 128
Hicks, Pvt. John W.	…128
Hire, Pvt. Chessley	…Ded., 128
Hitchcock, Clelland	…52
Hoffarth (Hofford), Orville A.	…Ded.,129
Hoover, Cpl. Cecil Ray	…52, 129
Hoover, Sgt. Frank Dave	…5, 6, 52, 54, 71, 94, 129
Hoover, Herbert	…11, 17
Hopewell, Apprentice Seaman Otho George	…129
Huggans, Roy Dickerson	…129
Hunt, Ault	…Ded.
Hunt, Jr., Seaman 2nd Class John W.	…Ded., 130
Hurst, Pvt. Zeek	…130
Hylton, Noah	…88
Ingraham, Sgt. Thomas Corvan	…Ded., 130
Ipock, Cpl. Walter Henry	…130
Jennings, Pvt. Sherman E.	…131
Johnson, Rev. L. A.	…98
Johnson, Cpl. Louis Wint	…Ded., 131
Keeling, Pvt. Ira Rutherford	…131
Keeling, Thomas Lovell	…16, 131
Kellogg, Pvt. Bertie	…132
Kendrick, Mr.	…20
Kester, Pvt. William Elmer	…132
King, Pvt. Clarence	…Ded., 2, 5, 6, 41, 52, 95, 98, 132
King, Elbert H.	…2, 52, 98, 132
King-Slate, Mary Jane	…2, 99, 132, 133
Lane, Rose Wilder	…79
Leroy, Pvt. Willie	…133
Liska, Pvt. Yaroslov	…Ded., 81, 133
Livingston, Harold	…51
Lovall, Marion	…20
Luttrell, Shelton C.	…133
Maberry, Hina	…51
Mashburn, Pvt. Joseph Davis	…65, 133
Mays, Pvt. Carl William	…68, 69, 70, 133

Mays, Cpl. Frank	...85, 134
McMurtrey, Pvt. Oliver Harvey	...Ded., 134
McMurtrey, Pvt. Virgil Monroe	...134
Miller, Pvt. Archie James	...86, 134
Miller, Raymond Kelton	...88, 135
Mingus, Lester E.	...5
Moody, Cpl. Harry Lester	...135
Mooney, Harry	...52
Moore, Pvt. John Austin	...135
Morris, Pvt. James Andrew	...36, 37, 136
Morris, Fred	...20
Morris, John	...36
Newton, Efton	...136
Newton, Pvt. Ezra Trimble	...136
Newton, Hosea Earl	...136
Newton, Ira "Jason"	...136
Newton, Jesse Albert	...137
Newton, Pvt. John Allison "Al"	...9, 95, 137
Newton, P. W.	...7
Newton, Pvt. William Moses "Mose"	...81, 95, 138
Newton, Cpl. Samma "Sam"	...137
Newton, Walter Dewey	...138
Norcross, Roy G.	...5, 6, 139
Oberholser, Harriett	...33
Oetting, "Grandpa"	...24
Packard, Ernest A.	...5, 139
Patterson, Rev. J. W.	...98
Peacock, Frank Leroy, Sr.	...139
Pershing, Major General John J. "Black Jack"	...Notes, 14, 23, 24, 35, 47
Phillips, Pvt. Burl	...139
Pierce, Lieut. Col. Charles C.	...3
Plaster, Pvt. Clarence	...Ded., 140
Poe, Sgt. Maj. Carlyle	...51, 140
Pope, Frank	...51, 140
Potts, John J.	...5, 6, 52, 94, 140
Renn, Oscar	...51
Reynolds, Mayor William G.	...7, 69, 80
Riley, Mayor F. H.	...6
Riley, Raymond Roy	...141
Rippee, Foster Asberry	...141
Rippee, Hosea Nichols	...141
Rippee, Pvt. Ira Eli	...141
Rippee, Verner	...52, 141
Robinett, Maj. Clifton Harvey	...50, 51, 142
Robinett, Brig. Gen. Paul McDonald	...95, 142
Roe, William Jonas "Joe"	...5, 142
Rogers, Dr. Robert M.	...33, 52, 142
Roosevelt, Edith	...Notes
Roosevelt, Pres. Theodore	...Notes
Roosevelt, Quentin	...Notes
Roote, Jr., Maj. Jesse B.	...51, 143
Roper, Pvt. Arthur William	...74, 143
Ross, Pvt. 1st Class Charles Sylvester	...143

Ross, Frank	...51
Ross, Jess	...17, 51
Rumple, Pvt. Roy Calvin	...143
Rush, Auda Doil	...144
Samuels, Pvt. George C.	...60, 144
Sanders, Isaac Newton	...74, 144
Sanders, Sheriff C. G.	...34
Schlicher, Pvt. 1st Class William Richard	...22, 25, 91, 144
Scott, Pvt. James Brodie	...Ded., 145
Seal, Pvt. Clifford Mark	...30, 71, 145
Seibold, Grace Darling	...97
Sellers, Cpl. Elmer Oliver	...Ded., 145
Sherrell, Pvt. Ora (Oron)	...145
Shores, Geo.	...78
Short, Herbert Anesworth	...52, 65, 74, 146
Short, Kathy	...Ack.
Shumate, Jason	...146
Sikes, William Everett	...147
Skelton, Pvt. James K. Polk	...147
Skiles, Pvt. James Warren	...Ded., 147
Smith, Pvt. George O. "Ola"	...147
Smith, Joe H.	...50
Smith, Noah C.	...88
Smith, Cpl. Owen Lewis	...148
Smith, Pvt. Robert	...148
Snow, Pvt. Henry Isaac	...Ded., 148
Spurlock, John "Ernie" Ernest	...5, 148
Stephens, Cpl. Harry B.	...17, 149
Stout, Ira Clarence	...48, 75, 84, 149
Street, Walter G.	...Ded.
Strong, Pvt. Elmer	...52, 149
Stubby	...59
Sutherland, Pvt. Lester Ray	...149
Tarbutton, Clyde	...5, 6, 40, 66, 77, 94, 95, 149
Tefteller, Pvt. James	...74, 150
Tester, Pvt. Leon Raymond	...Ded., 96, 150
Thorne, Sgt. Maynard Hall	...Ded., 81, 150
Todd, Cpl. Joseph Clarence	...150
Todd, Pvt. Joseph Maurice	...Ded.,151
Tool, Archie Walter	...Ded., 151
Tooley, Pvt. Roy W.	...151
Tripp, Claude Elmer	...5, 6, 9, 32, 33, 40, 77, 94, 152
Tripp, Orlando Karl	...52, 152
Turner, Pvt. Alva McKinley	...152
Turner, Carl Raymond	...153
Viles, Pvt. Robert C.	...5, 6, 153
Von Hindenburg, Gen. Paul	...47
Von Ludendorff, Erich	...53
Von Richthofen, Manfred Baron "the Red Baron"	...19
Wallace, Apprentice Seaman Claude Floran	...153
Westbrook, Ed.	...52
Westbrook, Inez	...78
Whitteker, Robert Reed	...5, 6, 153

Whittlesey, Major Charles White	…58
Whitwer, Edward	…51
Wilder, Mrs. A. J.	…51, 79
Wilhelm II, Kaiser	…7, 25, 47, 50
Williams, Harley S.	…88
Williams, Pvt. 1st Class James Ila	…74, 154
Wilson, Pres. Woodrow	…4, 35
Woodford, Pvt. William Oliver	…154
Wright, Frank A.	…Ded., 154
Yeager, Pvt. Otis	…Ded., 154
Young, Pvt. Floyd S.	…155
Young, PFC. Ira Elmer	…52, 155
Young, Pvt. 1st Class, Jesse Allen	…156
Young, Ray	…Ded., 156
Young, Pvt. Raymond	…52, 95, 156
Younger, Paul	…52

NOTES